Day Trading
With
My Hebrew Uncle

C. RANDLE VOYLES MD

First Edition 2019

This work is a blend of fact and creative memoir. Characters were embellished, some incidents were created, and specific dialogues were recorded as a function of the author's imagination and memory. Thus, any resemblance to persons or actual events may be coincidental. Unless otherwise indicated, Bible quotations are from the New Living Translation.

Cover designed by author.

Independently published.

ISBN: 9781731083029
ISBN-13:

DEDICATION

Solomon Avram Goldfarb
(1925-2009)

As a trader, he was ruthless.
As my uncle, he had a gentle heart.
He was an idealist
who became entangled in the crossroads of life.
He was an earnest Karaite.
He was my mentor.

CONTENTS

ACKNOWLEDGEMENT

THANKS TO MANY BUT MOSTLY TO
MY LOVING WIFE , CLOSEST FRIEND, AND
MY MOST FEROCIOUS EDITOR,
BETTY ANN

MANY OTHERS HELPED WITH REVIEW:

CHUCK, ANOTHER CHUCK, A CHARLES,
THOMAS, TOMMY (AND ANNA), MAT, LARRY,
LARRY LEO, JUDGE, MIKE, JASON, JOHNNY,
ELLEN ANN, GERRY, THE "BOSS," JAMES, JOHN,
GARY, TOBY, JIM, LANIS, STAN, BETTY, MELVIN,
ROBERT, JEFF, BECKY, ED…

1 THE BELLIGERENT CROWS

"Hey boy, do you hear that?"

"Hear what, Uncle Wilbur?"

"You're not listening, boy." He flicked my ear. "Hear that crunch… that crunch of gravel? That's gotta be your favorite uncle, the Hebrew peddler. He's a comin' up the road. Just listen."

***

You city folk might not appreciate it, but there is a distinctive crunch when an oncoming car rounds the curve of a recently-graded country road. I strained to hear it. My favorite uncle was about to arrive. To me, he was so special -- the smartest man in the world. His name: Solomon Avram Goldfarb. *Hebrew peddler?* Blame it on the naivety of an eight-year old; I did not sense an ethnic rub.

My blood-kin uncles were all gentile. Dirt farmers. Not rednecks per se but a bit short on refinement and polish. They eked out a meager living toiling under the sun, never venturing far from Route 2 in Tippah County near Falkner, Mississippi. In spite of their hard lives, they considered themselves bountifully blessed by the Good Lord.

Uncle Solomon was so different. He was fabulously wealthy and travelled the world. He traded cotton at the Memphis Cotton Exchange and gold at the New York COMEX. With tongue-in-cheek, he would chuckle and refer to himself as a scavenger of commerce or, yes, a glorified peddler.

1

Now as I reflect back, I cringe with the recall of another set of sounds. Years later... Yes, at least thirty years later. I was standing in that very same spot in front of the old home place. Car doors slamming followed by the roar of an engine. Spinning tires seeking traction. I heard that same crunch of gravel, but this time… this time fading in the distance. I didn't blame Uncle Solomon and his Egyptian lady friend for leaving. I knew he would never return. He had been openly insulted and rejected by my family, but not by me. For a moment, my world went quiet. I was stunned. Then, from high in the loblolly pines in the direction of Wicker Mountain, belligerent crows broke the silence. They cackled and cawed -- a prelude to a more caustic cacophony from inside the house. My aunts and uncles hovered around the red-checkered, oil-clothed kitchen table. Louder cackles. Louder caws. They were the more belligerent crows.

***

"She's a woman of the night!"

"Sister, she's a harlot!" said another.

"I'll bet Solomon picked her up on one of them high-end streets in Paris..."

"Sister, now she's his concubine."

"No, no, no! Sister, what you really mean is that she's just *one*… hear me, I said just one of his concubines."

"Y'all shush a minute," cried Uncle Wilbur as he stood and steadied himself, placing both hands on the kitchen table. Everyone was quiet. His one good eye began to bulge, a heralding sign of the mounting crescendo – a practice perfected in the pulpit. "You say woman of the night? Harlot? Concubine? No, I'll say it plain as day. In Tippah County…" He stopped to wipe his forehead with a red bandanna, "In Tippah County, I call her a gol-durned French whore."

After the shortest requisite pause in respect for her husband Wilbur, Aunt Maxine resumed the attack. "Ain't no telling how many women he keeps up at that gaudy Memphis mansion." She turned to me. "And Junior here, you had the gall to name that monstrosity Havilah, a name from the Lord's book of Genesis."[1]

---

[1] Genesis 2:10-12 NLT: *"A river flowed from the land of Eden… around the entire land of Havilah, where gold is found.*

2

"I will not hear of it!" I shouted. "Shame on you! Uncle Solomon deserves better than this. He is a real gentleman. You just resent his wealth. He could buy all of Tippah County."

BLAM! Uncle Wilbur's hand slapped the table. *"Lay not up for yourselves treasures upon earth, where moth and rust doth corrupt.* He may be rich in worldly terms but inside… I say inside he is just a glorified peddler. Y'all have heard it from Solomon his own self."

"You are not being fair to Uncle Solomon. He deserves the respect of this family. Uncle Wilbur, before you say he is not blood kin, let me ask where's the Good Samaritan in you?" I surveyed the room. No one had ever dared take a position at odds with Uncle Wilbur except, of course, Aunt Maxine. "Uncle Solomon is a kind man. He cares for his Egyptian lady friend. Not one of you gave her a chance. I agree that she is not like you. She is elegant, and she just happens to be the leading model in all of Paris. Please give Uncle Solomon a little credit." I turned directly to Aunt Maxine. "You told me about the tears he shed standing at Aunt Grace's grave at Pine Hill. As a young man, he vowed that he would never marry again. He's been a man of his word. There's nothing wrong with him having a little female companionship. You saw it. He is very close to her."

"I'll say close," interrupted Aunt Maxine. "He's close inside them Egyptian sheets."

"Shame on you," I continued. "You women are just jealous, and you men are just full of envy. As I said, shame on you."

BLAM! Uncle Wilbur again pounded the table. "Well just because you made a surgeon don't mean you know anything at all about right and wrong – especially for Tippah County. Let's make it clear! That French whore and her Hebrew sugar daddy ain't welcomed in this house again…"

***

WHOA!

Take a deep breath!

Imagine yourself in my seat. A surgeon, recently-turned-author, with a story to tell. My initial plan was to document how a financial plebe discovered a low-risk, high-return trading system in 1986 that lasted fourteen years[2]. However, the story grew bigger than that. The emphasis on finance shifted to personal psychology, and my number-crunching opus morphed into quasi-memoir. Memoir then transitioned to biography... that being my uncle's biography. Biographies, if they have any real value, should teach good lessons. I trust the lessons from his life are clearly portrayed as they reflect long-standing truths – dare I say, the verities of life. Now... imagine yourself in my seat.

No real story that encompasses several decades, if told honestly, is free of conflict. Of conflict, there was plenty. Critics might rightly accuse me of introducing fiction as I refuse to dwell on my uncle's shortcomings. We all have our flaws; my uncle had his. Just like in a card game, strength in one suit generally begets weakness in another. Besides, the grand jury declared that all of the evidence against him was just circumstantial.

My uncle taught me that a successful business may be measured by a balance sheet but true success in life cannot be defined with numbers. His teachings are time-tested and should be of interest to you even if you have no interest in finance. Alternatively, you may consider yourself a trading maestro blazing a new path; my uncle would declare your route is just a variant of something old. As he said so often to me...

There is nothing new under the sun.

---

[2] *[Stale prices and strategies for trading mutual funds. J Boudoukh, M Richardson, M Subrahmanyam, RF Whitelaw. Financial Analysts Journal 58 (4), 53-71 (July-August, 2003). [For further information, see John C. Bogle's *Don't Count on It!*, page 336-340; John Wiley and Sons, Hoboken, NJ (2011).]

2 OUT OF TIPPAH

(This chapter should be read with a rich Southern accent, i.e. Faulkner.)

No, we weren't poor by world standards. Not even poor for Tippah County. But from early on, I feared that destiny had me bound, even enslaved, by the limits of rural Tippah. No ball and chains needed; I would be bound by dirty work-boots. Don't get me wrong. There is nothing wrong with work or work-boots… or dirt. I just sought a different path.

Tippah County – a small county in Northeast Mississippi – was not the Mississippi of grand plantations with rich alluvial soils, antebellum homes, and landed gentry. The hill country was largely spared the stain and sin of slavery, as Tippah was primarily inhabited by poor white farmers who lived off the soil by the sweat of their brow. Life in Tippah County was an isolated existence – *cut off* from so much of the world. Appropriately, *Tippah* is a Chickasaw word meaning "cut off." It was no surprise that a diaspora occurred after World War II. Returning soldiers – having been exposed to the urban world – left Tippah in droves, leading to a 25% reduction in the county's population within two decades. Poor whites moved to Memphis; blacks migrated to points farther north.

For many of the remaining young veterans, sharecropping provided an unkind and crude substitute for formal education. A land owner leased his field and loaned money towards the crop; the sharecropper provided the labor. After the crop was harvested, the farmer first paid a rental fee and any other borrowed money plus interest to the landowner. *Usurious* may not have been a common word of Tippah vocabulary, but it was of practice. Finally, the farmer and landowner split any residual profit. After experiencing the futility of sharecropping, my father followed the family trail to Memphis.

As first-generation migrants to the city, we always reconvened on special holidays at the family home place, about two miles of dirt road from the railway station at Falkner, Mississippi. The small community was named for the businessman, Colonel William C. Falkner, who built the Ripley Railroad after the Civil War. The Colonel died as a result of a gunshot wound inflicted by a disgruntled business partner named Thurmond. [Although the county was thinly populated, we cannot identify a bloodline to the Colonel; we are more likely related to his assailant.] By the way, the Colonel wrote several novels and he was also the great-grandfather of a Nobel Prize-winning author who added a "u" to his name.

It was at the home place that I have my first memory of my Uncle Solomon. I wonder if he knew what an influence his seemingly casual remarks would have on an attentive nephew that day. My recollections are clear. It was hot. The air was so thick that I was reminded of yesterday's fresh-caught bream gulping on the creek bank. Under the shade of the family red oak, six or seven would-be patriarchs were re-telling those countless "remember-when" stories. Two uncles smoked Lucky Strikes; another chewed Red Man. A pesky buzzing horse fly added to the misery.

"Dang-it, that horse fly bit me!"

Happily, I heard the soothing drone of crushing ice as two kegs of homemade ice cream were in the making; hand-cranked, of course.

'Don't turn that crank too fast. The ice cream will never make," instructed an uncle. "Add a little more rock salt."

Although I might have seemed distracted by my childhood pursuit of a doodlebug, I listened and heard every word from Uncle Solomon.

"The key to business is a good understanding of math and science... and then psychology. To succeed as a trader, you have to know your strength and your adversaries' weakness. There are always opportunities. But never forget: true success in life is measured by more than numbers on a balance sheet."

I have a special memory of that statement as I now protect the old books from his extensive collection. His library included most of the works of our neighborhood author William Faulkner. Inside the cover of *Absalom, Absalom* was his handwritten Faulkner quote. *You cannot swim for new horizons until you have the courage to lose sight of the shore.* Underneath the note was another scribble of Faulkner fame: *Shoot high… Try to be better than yourself.* His collection also included Charles Darwin's *The Power of Movement of Plants* from 1880; inside the cover was an intriguing note:

> *Would love to tease Darwin with the mystery of my vining wisteria.*
> *Charlie boy, which way doth the vine twine?*
> *And why?*
> *SAG, 1965*

Why would an already successful businessman study such? He provided his answer with a cherished note inside a dusty calculus book cover:

> *Education is an open-ended process.*
> *Lifelong.*
> *There are no specific end-points.*
> *Numbers count.*
> *SAG, 1971*

Uncle Solomon was not a dirt farmer. Never had been. A different ancestry. But, maybe not completely…

***

Looking back as an eight-year-old

Tippah County did not provide much diversity in my youth. Yes, we had both Methodists and Baptists. We were the variant known as Primitive Baptists: "foot washers" like Jesus; "hard-shelled" like St. Paul. [According to the biblical account in John 13, Jesus washed the feet of his disciples.] As a point of nomenclature, our charter members in the early 1800s chose the word "primitive" to convey the sense of "original," suggesting that our divining roots preceded the Catholic church. To make the point more clearly, all church singing was *a cappella* – no piano or instruments. "Had we needed instruments in the church, Christ would have said it," explained Uncle Wilbur.

Pine Hill Primitive Baptist Church, Highway 502, Falkner, Mississippi. Yes, a small white church on a hill blanketed by southern loblolly pines. Cemetery across the road. Family graves dating back to the original settlers among the Chickasaw Indians. An age-speckled tombstone marked the sacrifice of John C. Norton CSA, confederate soldier, age 18. There were no Catholic churches. No Jewish synagogues. The study of Islam and Buddha may have been introduced in social studies, but I have no such memory. You were either a Believer or something akin to a communist. In the midst of the homogeneous Christian culture, I found it a bit strange – when right after capturing my first doodlebug – that I first heard Uncle Solomon proclaim to everyone: "Never forget our shared Hebrew heritage..."

Our shared Hebrew heritage? What is my uncle talking about?

Uncle Solomon's family business featured high-end clothing imported from Europe with distribution across the South. For reasons initially unknown to me, he had become estranged from his family of third generation immigrant Jews. At first, I was told that his family strife was due to his marriage to my Aunt Grace outside of Judaism. However, it was not that simple. As I learned later, Uncle Solomon was the biological product of an extra-marital relationship between his father David and his young secretary who, in addition to being gentile, was married to the leading Goldfarb traveling salesman. Bitter divorces and re-assigned "job descriptions" were followed by even more disharmony in the Memphis tribe of Judah. Father David provided financial support but little nurture as a parent; you see, he divorced his not-now-so-hot princess soon after delivery. Thus, my Uncle Solomon was labelled a Goldfarb but, for practical purposes, he was born to a single mother, referred to by her own family as the slut with an illegitimate Jew-boy.

In his childhood, my Uncle Solomon was treated like a leper by his older Jewish half-brother, Adonijah Aaron Goldfarb. In Hebrew, Adonijah means "the Lord is my God," but his friends called him "Double A" which evolved to "Double A, the Wicked One," which was further shortened to "Wicked." Wicked created a progression of nicknames for his resented half-brother. Early on, he called him *shaygitz*, which is Yiddish for a male gentile.

In his teenage years, the name-calling was more caustic. First came *mamzer* (Yiddish for bastard child) and then came *son of nafka* (Yiddish for whore) which evolved to the simple: "Whore Boy, Whore Boy, Whore Boy." Young Solomon grew up as a never-accepted child; a half-breed to the Jews, a tainted boy to the gentiles.

In things intellectual, he excelled; in personal relationships, not so much. As a lonely child, he turned his energy to his studies. He became enthralled with Jewish history and, in particular, the writings associated with his namesake, King Solomon, who was recorded to be the wisest and most wealthy king of his time. Like King Solomon, he was attracted to the arts and he became a master violinist. To escape the turmoil in Memphis, his mother arranged travel to Europe every summer and he became fluent in French. She did her best to protect him, and she was determined that her baby boy get an appropriate share of the Goldfarb business. However, after a childhood of misery, Uncle Solomon knew that peaceful resolution was hopeless. When he finished college, he took what was intended to be a demeaning Goldfarb assignment in Alexandria, Egypt. In the multicultural environment, Solomon flourished. He traded for the finest Egyptian cotton for transfer to Paris where cousin Fritz Goldfarb oversaw the production of the family's clothing and bedding. Solomon traveled often to Paris; he and Fritz became the closest of friends. However, the Memphis quagmire never improved. The inevitable conflict came to a boil when Father David died after a long struggle with Parkinson's disease.

Upon arrival in Memphis for his father's funeral, Solomon grimaced at Wicked's greeting: "Welcome back, Whore Boy." Two days later, the will was read. Uncle Solomon received a token interest in the family business. He demanded to be bought out and accepted the initial offer, even though it was a fraction of its value.

"What did you expect, Whore Boy?" asked Wicked.

Little did either of them know, but that was their last verbal exchange, unusual in that Memphis was such a small town for Jewish half-brothers.

Uncle Solomon took his paltry settlement from the family business and soon became the most prominent and feared trader at the Memphis Cotton Exchange. On review, one might conclude that his loner childhood filled with strife and coated with cynicism prepared him well for cut-throat trading. At the same time, the Goldfarb Fabric import business dwindled as

Double A the Wicked became engrossed in a life of misdirection, resorting to excessive gambling and alcohol.

Not content with prominence in the cotton trade, Uncle Solomon ventured into the gold trade and, once again, was met with enormous success. Always the pragmatic academic, he published insightful editorials in the literature of international finance. Though personally shy and introverted, he took on a practiced exuberance at the podium and became a sought-after speaker. One of his favorite academic topics was the historic similarity of the trade of cotton and gold. I was too young to appreciate the content which he tried to share with our Tippah family, but I do remember one of his statements for his lecture in Paris:

"Gold may have been the mortar that built cathedrals of Europe… but cotton built the South."

At family gatherings, he would espouse the virtues of Egyptian cotton. And cotton, he really knew. He brought Egyptian pillowcases for all of my aunts: *the world's finest cotton, 500 thread count.* We all enjoyed pictures from his travels. Riding a camel in front of the pyramids. Standing in front of the Sphinx.

"I have traveled much of the world, but the warmest place in my heart, besides Tippah county, of course, is Alexandria, Egypt." He leaned over to me. "Someday you will visit historic Alexandria. You'll see what I mean."

My youthful recollection was that he was loved unconditionally by our family. Maybe it was an aberration, but it seemed to make no difference - even in rural Mississippi - that he was not actual blood kin or that he was a Jew. He had loved his young wife, my Aunt Grace, and visited her grave frequently in spite of the passing years. When called on to bless the food, Uncle Solomon ended his prayer "in Jesus name we pray." A hearty "amen" from my deacon uncles was then echoed to completion by Uncle Wilbur – a World War II veteran awarded a Purple Heart in Belgium. He had a terrible facial injury. Lost his left eye. Now a farmer and lay minister at Pine Hill. Uncle Wilbur's dress was Sunday best: sun-faded but clean overalls; plaid shirt. In that era, the women made their own dresses, usually with a calico print. By contrast, Uncle Solomon's attire was that of a sophisticated gentleman. Urban, even with a European flair. I admired his linen jacket. Crisp white shirt. Thin necktie of the fifties era. A simple tie pin featuring a cotton boll – solid gold, by my assessment. The handkerchief in his left coat pocket matched his tie. Well-cropped thin mustache. And the aroma of the cherry tobacco from his ivory pipe!

"Solomon, why don't you get out your fiddle and play us a concert," urged Uncle Wilbur at the end of the day, never appreciating the difference between fiddles and violins... nor those who played them.

The music of our Welsh/Irish heritage had become even more deeply ingrained along immigrant trails across Appalachia. Accordingly, Uncle Solomon played our rendition of country, bluegrass, and gospel.

"Sol, play 'Amazing Grace' one more time." Uncle Wilbur asked predictably. "You know it so good."

What a splendor of sound! As Uncle Solomon danced his bow across the strings of his violin, his eyes watered.

"Mama, why does Uncle Solomon tear up when he plays that sad song?" I asked that night.

"It's because the song reminds him of Aunt Grace's funeral."

Only later—when they sang it at Grandma Nance's funeral—did I realize that "Amazing Grace" was not a direct reference to my *Amazing* Aunt Grace.

***

To me, Uncle Solomon was neither pretentious nor condescending as he offered intellectual comment, but he seemed to struggle with ordinary conversation. I wondered if his apparent unease was a function of his difficult childhood. Even his body language seemed stilted... almost unnatural... something you can't grow out of. When he made a special point, he took on what seemed to be a practiced posture raising his left eyebrow and palming his pipe. Looking back, he reminded me of my distinguished but awkwardly disjointed professors I had in medical school. His enunciation was just too structured and overly precise, that is, for Tippah County, Route 2.

"Remember our shared Hebrew heritage..." he explained to my uncles with eyebrow raised, "but we have to speak well to uphold the legacy of our neighborhood author, William Faulkner."

He followed with a whisper to me: "Dear Plimenik, never forget... our shared Hebrew heritage... and Faulkner... Never forget... They are part of us."

"But Uncle Sol, why do you call me *Plimenik?*" I whispered back.

"It's my special name for my favorite nephew."

"How do you spell that word?"

Leaning closer: "P-L-I-M-E-N-I-K."

"I've never heard that I had Hebrew ancestors. Uncle Sol, what do you mean?"

He showed a gratifying smile and said "Yes, the Hebrew played an important role in Welsh and Irish heritage. I can't wait until you're a little older. We will discuss it all in due time."

"One other thing, Uncle Sol, who is Faulkner?"

"William Faulkner is probably the greatest author to ever come out of Mississippi. He wrote about something simple, yet complex. He wrote about conflict of the human soul. He earned famous national awards as well as the Nobel Prize in literature in 1949.

"But Uncle Sol, what is the Nobel Prize?" (Remember, I was just 8 years old.)

***

Back in Memphis. Just off Lamar Avenue. You might call it a starter home today. Two bedrooms/one bath. Four kids at our house. No air-conditioner. Roaring ceiling fan with screened windows. Small white box of a refrigerator with those metal ice trays. Red fly swatters. The neighbors all touted similar stories – just different nouns with predictable adjectives. Loyal Veterans. Dedicated Americans. Mr. Jones had been a buck sergeant. Most had lesser ranks. *I was a greasy sailor, the South Pacific. I was a grunt soldier in France.* They were all white. All from rural locales. All hopeful of a better life. It still amazes me that – in spite of their recent move to the city – the collective chorus was that there's no place like home. Where were these glorious home places, you might ask? *We lived just outside of…* Lambert or Jug Fork in Mississippi or near Haleyville or Nevertell in Alabama. In that time, where you went to the *picture show* was the generally-accepted geographic landmark.

I asked Mother to take me to the city library.

***

"Could you help me, Mrs. Gravner. I am looking for a special word. I have already looked in the Merriam-Webster dictionary as well as the Oxford English dictionary. I can't find my word."

Mrs. Gravner, the librarian, had always been so helpful in my trips to the Memphis library. "Of course, I will help you. What is your word?"

"It's a word from my uncle. It is spelled P-L-I-M-E-N-I-K. I am certain that it is spelled correctly but I cannot find any trace of it in our dictionaries," I replied.

She chuckled and her smile broadened. "Well, you must have an interesting uncle and he must think that you are very special. You see, *plimenik* is a Yiddish word for nephew. I didn't realize that you were Jewish."

"I don't think I'm Jewish, but I think my uncle is. What do you mean by the word *Yiddish*?" (Again, I'm the 8 years old product of Tippah, the cut-off county.)

"Yiddish is a language used by immigrant Jews from Germany and Eastern Europe. Jews from that area are generally referred to as Ashkenazic Jews. The Jews from Spain, Portugal, and Mediterranean area are called Sephardic Jews. The Yiddish dialect mixed words from Hebrew, German, and several other modern languages. *Yiddish* is the Yiddish word for Jewish."

"Mrs. Gravner, why did you know so much when the Oxford English dictionary did not?" I asked.

She smiled at me.

"It's part of my culture."

"So, you must be Yiddish?" I asked.

She smiled again.

"One final question," I said. "What is the Yiddish word for uncle?"

"That would be *feter*... spelled F-E-T-E-R."

"Mrs. Gravner, do you know anything about Egyptian cotton?"

"Egyptian is the finest cotton... the cotton that gives you cloth with a 500-thread count."

***

Once back at home, I immediately asked to call my uncle. Once the party line cleared, my mother dialed his number. "Goldfarb Cotton. How can I help you?" I overheard the secretary's voice. Mother asked for Mr. Goldfarb and gave me the phone.

"Uncle Sol, guess who this is?"

"My first guess is that this is a delightful young man named Plimenik," he said. "And how do you like your name?"

"I love it, Uncle Sol. Thank you for being so special to me. And I think you will like your new name," I said. "From now on, you are Feter to me… Feter Sol!"

"Plimenik, how did you find that name?" he asked.

"From the city librarian. Her name is Mrs. Gravner. She is Yiddish," I said. "She knows a lot of things… even about Egyptian cotton."

3 COTTON, CADILLACS AND RUBIES

Growing up, age 17.
July 4, 1967.
Tippah County, home place.

The past decade had brought little change. The patriarchs repeated the same old stories… and laughed again. As before, the giant red oak tree provided little relief from the heat of the midday sun. Aunt Maxine had planted a wisteria near the base of the oak tree and its vines crawled up the trunk, claiming their space. The old hand-cranked ice cream maker was gone, having been replaced by Uncle Wilbur's new whining electrical unit. I was following instructions to add more rock salt when I heard that distinctive crunch of gravel from an oncoming car. Uncle Solomon had arrived.

"Gol-durn! Would you look at that," bellowed Uncle Wilbur. He spat out his Red Man. His fellow patriarchs stood in unison as if on order like the congregation at Pine Hill.

I ran into the house. "Mama, y'all come out quick. Uncle Solomon is here. He's driving a brand-new Cadillac. It's a convertible. It's ruby red. It's the prettiest car I've ever seen." All of the women and their swarm of children emptied onto the front yard. What irony! America's most flashy car – Tippah's most dusty road.

Perhaps I should offer some more background. My Aunt Grace (Uncle Solomon's wife) was in her second trimester of pregnancy in late 1949… as was my mother with me. Both pregnant sisters looked forward to decorating the home place for Christmas, a shared experience dating back to their adolescence.   Unfortunately, Aunt Grace was driving alone to the home place and had a head-on collision on highway 72. She was killed instantly. Uncle Solomon carried a cloak of guilt for the rest of his life. Many years later, he confided in me and told me of his last words to his young wife: *Gracie, I don't know why we need to leave a day early just so that you and your sister can put out even more Christmas decorations. I have a business to run and I have a major trade on. If it's so important to you, go on by yourself.* In his grieving period, he purchased an identical shiny black 1947 Chevrolet. Uncle Solomon rarely drove the Chevy, usually just to visit the grave site. He named his car *Mrs. Gracie.* You now may understand why Uncle Solomon treated me like a son.

"Uncle Solomon, it's gorgeous," I said as I gave him a welcoming hug.

"It's just a car. It provides transportation from point A to point B. But…" he paused, "she is pretty. She comes with a lesson. Your Aunt Grace would want me to drive the Cadillac today. Now help me get these boxes out of the trunk. I just got back from Paris. I have bed sheets for the whole family. Egyptian cotton. 500 thread count. The best in the world."

I leaned up next to Uncle Sol and whispered, "Feter Sol, I love your new car. Now I am *really* ready to learn more about trading cotton… maybe gold too."

"I know you are eager, Plimenik. Today you will get your first lesson. If you understand cotton, you will understand the history of Mississippi and much of America. If you understand gold, you will understand the history of the world. Before you approach trading either cotton or gold, you need to understand yourself."

I was perplexed but not surprised by the nature of his response. I was also disappointed when all of my young cousins interrupted our conversation. "Let's go for a ride, Uncle Sol. Take us for a ride."

"Not now, dear ones. There will be time for joyriding after dinner. Let me visit with your parents. I have new pictures from Egypt."

***

After what seemed forever, dinner (the noon meal in the rural South) was finally blessed and served. We had the usual Southern fare: country ham, fried chicken, sweet potatoes, potato salad, purple-hulled peas and such.

"This ham is the best I have ever had," said Uncle Sol.

"Thank you, Sol," said Uncle Wilbur. "It's the best of Tippah: salt-cured and hickory-smoked right here in our own smokehouse."

The adults ate in the dining room, but the kids scattered throughout the house. I ate on the front porch swing where I could admire Uncle Sol's new car. After homemade ice cream, the focus immediately went back to the car. "Take us for a ride, Uncle Sol. Take us for a ride."

Uncle Sol adhered to his promise that everyone could ride. I remember the waning crunch of gravel as the ruby-red beauty departed for the turn-around point at the Falkner train station. After the final trip (Aunt Maxine declared that she was always last), Uncle Solomon took me aside and whispered: "It's time for you to drive. Let's begin your first lesson in trading."

With Uncle Solomon, I knew there was a serious message but my youthful eagerness to drive precluded any such thought. I was struck by that new car smell – well apparent even in the open convertible. I turned on the ignition. The engine purred. I shifted into first gear. I reveled in the grandeur of the moment, paying as little attention to the envious stares of my cousins as I did to the layered dust on the kudzu. The car seemed to float over the ruts of the dusty road. Gravel crunched under the whitewalls and I winced as the errant rock dinged the Cadillac soft underside. After arriving at the train station, I put the car in neutral. That's when Uncle Sol reached over and turned off the motor. The purr was gone. Now quiet, save the cawing of some crows in the distant pines. We overlooked a pasture. A dozen Holstein cows resting in the shade of the day. Chewing their cud. Two looked our way.

"Feter Sol, thanks for letting me drive. Your new car is special," I said.

"What appears so real, so often, betrays the truth." He took out his pipe and added cherry tobacco. I recognized the heralding signs of a Feter Sol soliloquy. "Given the chance, we mortals create more favorable images for ourselves than we deserve. We all have shifting facades... façades that may cast no shadow of reality." Uncle Sol surveyed the horizon. I knew he was not thinking about the Holsteins. "Don't be misled by what seems obvious. Think independently. Cynicism and skepticism are frequently good traits. Develop your own conclusions." The still of the moment was again interrupted by the belligerent crows. "Back to the question, what's so special about this car? Be careful with your answer." He took a puff off his pipe, giving me time to think. "Remember what Leonardo da Vinci said: 'the most difficult opinion to correct is your own.'"

"I'm sorry, Feter. I am missing something," I said.

"Plimenik, do you like this car?"

"Of course, I like this car. It's probably the nicest car made in America."

"Well Plime', this is just a car… but it's not my car. My car is Mrs. Gracie, the 1947 Chevrolet. This is not my car."

"I'm even more confused, Feter Sol. Why are you driving it if it's not yours?"

"I am driving it to demonstrate your first lesson. Let me tell a story. It is painfully true." He palmed his pipe then took a puff. A wisp of smoke hung in the air.

"We recently hired a young trader in our firm. Recent Ole Miss graduate. Fraternity boy. Extremely bright, but poorly mannered. His family was from that old-monied group of self-proclaimed aristocrats of the South. They call themselves planters, not farmers. His daddy was one of my biggest clients, so I gave his son a job. They owned vast stretches of cotton land near Kruger. By the way, his real name was Joab, so he liked to be called Kruger." He raised his left eyebrow – the equivalent of adding bold italics to the spoken word. "You might say young Kruger was abundantly gifted with self-assurance – too confident in his competence. You should have heard him on his very first day. 'Mister Goldfarb,' he said. 'I trade cotton using modern technical tools called stochastics, relative strength index and Fibonacci retracement. Your trading based on weather forecasts and crop yield is antiquated. With my technical analysis, *we* can predict future prices. I will show you. Memphis will be just a stepping stone for me.'"

Uncle Solomon re-lit his pipe. I enjoyed the smell of the cherry tobacco. "In his first two weeks, Kruger caught a lucky streak, betting that the cotton price would go down.[3] I'll never forget his swagger of triumph as he marched into the lobby of the Peabody Hotel where he bought drinks for his surly friends. I know, because I followed him and listened from

---

[3] Betting that the market will go down is called shorting. The problem with shorting is that your losses are unlimited if the price goes up. Accordingly, when you short, you must set an exit point – what we call a stop – to limit your losses.

behind one of the granite columns. The whiskey flowed. Kruger toasted himself. 'Here's to Kruger; destiny is on his side. He will be the greatest cotton trader at Goldfarb.' With that announcement, fate would have it that he piqued the interest of a real-life devil who was infesting the Peabody happy hour."

"Who would that be, Feter Sol?"

"It was my old half-brother, Adonijah Aaron. You have never met him. Hopefully, you never will. He loves his nickname 'Wicked.' Wicked bought a new round of Makers Mark, encouraging Kruger to continue. That's when Kruger bragged about starting flying lessons and buying his new car. 'She's a ruby-red Cadillac. A convertible, no less. I named her *Miss Ruby*.'"

"Feter Sol, he seemed to be consumed with himself."

"That he was, but it was only temporary. You see, he was polishing a superficial façade, but his foundation was weak. I knew the market would teach him a painful lesson. You must understand that the display of exuberance in this business typically heralds impending disaster, especially for the novice who claims a new vision."

"What happened?"

"I called him into my office the next day and chastised him for talking *our* business to the bar crowd at the Peabody. I called him the *Mouth of the South*. I then suggested that he lighten his position in cotton, knowing that he would not listen. I was actually setting him up for what I knew would be his next response: he challenged me with a side bet that I was wrong. That's when I suggested that the wager should include the use of his new car."

Uncle Solomon paused and seemingly surveyed the horizon.

"Plime', cotton prices surged last week. Kruger suffered a devastating loss. When the market closed, he sought refuge at the lobby of the Peabody. There were no toasts to Kruger or his destiny. This time, Wicked bought more Makers Mark as he tried to milk him for information. Kruger was subdued. You know we mortals tend to brag about our successes and gloss over our failures. The next day, young Kruger had to call Daddy to bail him out." Uncle Solomon paused and surveyed the horizon. The crows cawed, the cows mooed. I listened.

"Now Plimenik, learn from the mistakes of others. Youthful enthusiasm, greed and short-term good fortune fuel pride. Pride bought the title to Miss Ruby. But look, Plimenik is driving the ruby trophy."

I sat silently. Uncle Solomon was a wise man who commanded respect in every crowd. Even the Holsteins seemed to be listening.

"Plimenik, you are my favorite nephew, as close as a son. As you know, I have been fairly successful in the modern trading world but I have lived with personal flaws. Just as my trading methods are not new, my personal flaws are ancient. Ancient Hebrew laws form the backbone of our culture and outline the path to a disciplined and successful life. If you follow those laws, you will be right, fair, and just most of the time."

He freshened his pipe and took a puff. He then reached into the glove box and took out a small three-ringed binder. "I am preparing a collection of rules for you. These are trading rules, but they have broader application; they are guiding principles of life." He handed me the binder. The cover was engraved **Hebrew Proverbs from Feter Solomon.** I opened the binder. It contained three pages.

#1 *Wisdom is more precious than rubies...*
Mishlei 3:15

"Feter Sol, you drove Miss Ruby, rather than Mrs. Gracie, to demonstrate a teaching point: wisdom is preferred to any shiny stone or flashy car. Aunt Gracie would be proud of you. "

"Plimenik, the lesson is not new. It is as ancient as Kruger's behavior. You see, Kruger set his own trap. Greed and pride were the bait. Greed may lead to short-term personal gain but obscures wisdom; pride generally robs people of true joy. In the end, Kruger lost his pride as well as a pile of his family's wealth. He had to eat the bitter fruit that he alone prepared. Do you know the word *schadenfreude*"?

"Sounds German," I replied.

"*Schadenfreude* is a German word that means deriving pleasure out of others' grief. I must confess that I hid my smile watching him choke on his own scheme. I know I shouldn't have, but I gave Kruger that same message in a glass frame: 'Wisdom is more precious than rubies.' You should have seen him. He threw the frame against the wall, cracking the glass. Kruger said nothing. Didn't have to. His hostile eyes said it louder than words: 'I'll-get-you-back, you son-of-a-b____.'"

Uncle Solomon reached over and turned to the second page.

#2 *Wisdom is more profitable than silver,*
And her wages are better than gold.
Mishlei 3:14

"Plimenik, to re-emphasize number one, gold and silver have been measures of wealth since the beginning of time. Wisdom and knowledge generally determine who accumulates silver and gold... but not always. However, a wealth of knowledge pays more predictable returns than a knowledge of wealth."

He turned to the third page.

#3 *The beginning of wisdom is the fear of the Lord.*
Mishlei 1:7

"Now, how does one obtain wisdom?" He took a more generous signature pause. I was digesting the content, much like the Holsteins re-chewing their cud. "Wisdom comes from honor, respect, and fear of the Lord. In spite of current views, Providence dictates that there are absolute rights and wrongs in this life. God provided an early framework through the Ten Commandments. They form the background for all our current laws. However, here's the problem. It is essentially impossible to trade commodities successfully and respect these instructions of the Lord. For certain, I have failed... and failed miserably. You see, trading commodities, such as cotton and gold, is a zero-sum game. By that, I mean my gains are a result of someone else's loss. More accurately, if someone else doesn't lose, I don't win." He lit his pipe, giving me a chance to re-digest, like a Holstein. "Do you understand?"

"Yes, I think so," I answered.

"In Tippah County vernacular, 'this ain't Sunday school.' The trading world is made up of conflict... conflict between buyers and sellers. Even if we don't have a position, my brokerage firm takes a commission on every trade, so we like heavy trading. We encourage the conflict. But Plime', trading is just a metaphor for conflict in life. You can't avoid it. Our neighborhood author, William Faulkner, perfected his literary art around that very subject. He said 'the only thing worth writing about is the human heart in conflict with itself.'"

Uncle Sol added tobacco to his pipe. I sat quietly.

"Plime', you are at a critical point in your life. I find it gratifying that you have interests in my line of business, but I am just a glorified peddler and I come from a long line of peddlers. For now, you need to focus on the beginning of wisdom and supplement that with math and science. I would urge you to develop a career where you help others rather than just serve yourself. I often wonder if I missed the mark early on. I would love to have a second life as a college professor or a physician where I could be a mentor to young intellects at their most creative point in life… For me right now, that's why my mentorship role with you is so special. You are smart and insightful. I urge you to keep your options open. Don't try to commit to anything for now but the path for wisdom. Opportunities will make themselves available to you."

I have little recollection of the dusty drive back to the home place. The ruby-red Cadillac was just a tool that my uncle used to teach me a lesson of life.

A few days later, I received an envelope from Goldfarb Cotton. Inside were three pages. The first was a simple handwritten note from my uncle: "Plimenik, like Faulkner suggested, I am a conflicted man. I am ashamed that I generated such a vicious sentiment toward Kruger. Please don't follow my example." The second page, already three-hole punched, was obviously intended for my three-ring binder:

> **#4 Don't rejoice when your enemy falls;**
> **don't be happy when they stumble.**
> **for the Lord will be displeased...**
> *Mishlei 24:17-18*

The third page was a cursive note.

> **#5 Priorities of life:**
> **GOD, Family, business, games...**
> **And in that order!**
> **Feter Sol, July 4, 1967**

When I returned to Memphis, I immediately went to the city library. Again, Merriam-Webster and the Oxford dictionaries were no help. I sought out my old friend. "Mrs. Gravner, I have another word that I cannot find in the dictionaries. It's from my Uncle Solomon – remember, Feter Sol. I think he may be using another Yiddish word."

"Have you been teased by that Yiddish uncle again?" She chuckled. "You know I'm more than happy to help you if I can. What is your word?"

"The word is *Mishlei*, spelled M-I-S-H-L-E-I."

"Mishlei is a Hebrew word, a word that means proverbs. Depending on the context, he may have been referring to a book in Jewish Scripture. Did he refer to any number with Mishlei?"

"It's funny that you ask. Each time he used the word, it was followed by a number," I answered.

"The number refers to a specific chapter of Scripture. What we call our Scripture is the same as your Old Testament. Many traditional Jews, perhaps most, rely on their rabbi to interpret the ancient text. Your uncle appears to be a self-directed student of Scripture. By the way, there is a sect of Jews who study the original verse, ignoring rabbinical extrapolation and the Talmud; they are called Karaite Jews. *Karaite* is a Hebrew word for *reader*."

***

The more I learned about my Fetor Sol, the more I cherished his advice and mentorship. He had shared with me his deepest and most thoughtful introspection. Not surprisingly, I started my college studies focused on mathematics and science. My career path included medical school and a surgical residency followed by an oncology fellowship in London. I then accepted a surgical position in Jackson, Mississippi. My interests remained academically-oriented as I published numerous papers and book chapters.

At the same time that I was graced with the *nobility* of the surgeon's challenge, I stumbled upon a sideline interest that was, at least culturally and emotionally, a diametrical opposite. I wallowed in the underbelly of international finance: hard-nosed; winner-take-all; take-no-prisoners. *This ain't Sunday school.* Under the direction of my uncle, I developed a trading strategy that was initially sparked by a small pricing inefficiency in gold.

Some would proclaim my efforts as laudable; others might malign me as an opportunist, a greed-driven speculator or even a scavenger of commerce. In view of my fondness for my mentor, I actually would prefer to be called the peddler's nephew.

On to gold!

4 THE RABBIT TRAIL TO GOLD

Almost two decades later.
November, 1986.
My age: 36 years.
Challenging, gratifying surgical career.
Jackson, Mississippi

"Feter Sol, got a minute?" I asked on a morning phone call.

"Plimenik, I always have time for you, even during trading hours."

"This is a different kind of phone call this morning. I have discovered something new. It may be the holy grail," I paused. He said nothing. "The holy grail of gold investing."

"I love your enthusiasm, but you must stand in line. You're the third person today to discover the holy grail. I am surrounded by either genius or naivety…" Uncle Solomon chuckled. "By the way, cotton is getting slammed today, but we are on the right side."

I could tell by the tone of his voice that he had a winning trade. I had learned over the years to limit my conversation when the market was going against him.

"I have consistently taken your advice about devoting my creative energy and passion to my career. I love the daily challenge of surgery. I love teaching and mentorship." I paused and chose my words carefully. "However, I have always craved the excitement of your trading."

"It's just a peddler's game… Nothing more. Now, get to your point," he interrupted. "What's on your mind?"

"Feter Sol, I followed your financial advice and put my little retirement account in the broad-based Stellar Fund based on that annual

25

Forbes report. However, I've been listening to TV commercials touting the safety of gold. At half-past every hour, Myron Kandel comes on CNN and announces the gold price. It's going up. And have you heard of Howard Ruff? He wrote a gold book called *Ruff Times*. Well, I have been studying a brand-new gold mutual fund; their portfolio…"

"Hold on. You're rambling and we are in trading hours," he interrupted. "Surely you should be using your time for something more noble than analyzing a gold mutual fund."

"But hear me out, Feter Sol. There is something bizarre about this fund. The daily price of the fund doesn't keep up with what's happening to the real-time price of gold. There's a screw-up somewhere. That's what I'm calling about. There seems to be a one-day lag. I'm thinking it's ripe for exploitation."

"Now Plime', help me understand. I deal with stocks, options, and futures. Traders don't deal with mutual funds. Those funds are the instruments of boring retirement plans. Tell me more," he said.

I explained that the traded shares of gold mining companies usually move up -- or down – two to three percent for every one percent change in the price of gold. A gold mutual fund contains shares of selected gold mining companies. This gold mutual fund appeared to have an error in how the managers arrived at the end-of-day asset price. The price was stale, at least by several hours compared to the spot price of gold and other gold funds.

"Plimenik, I don't mean to curb your enthusiasm, but there are many factors in successful trading. Knowing you, your observation is likely correct, but I would backfill with more information. I am always reluctant to offer this question, but do you have a large enough database to define an inefficiency?"

"Feter Sol, my surgical mentor had a favorite saying: 'If you have a stack of 100 bricks and you throw them out the window one at a time and just one brick goes up, that is significant.' It looks like the bricks are going up on a daily basis."

Traders make their living by exploiting pricing inefficiency. The inefficiency may occur from misguided emotions, better information, better analysis, or something as simple as mathematical miscalculations. High frequency trading is a more recent example where time-based advantage is exploited to less than a microsecond. While the markets are not always efficient, they work out inefficiency with a surprising speed. In the late 1980s, there was a flurry of activity as mutual fund companies developed new products. Commissions, or "loads," were reduced or eliminated entirely as competing funds tried to grow assets under management. As a further inducement, some family of funds even offered unlimited exchanges into and out of their funds. In the 1990s, platforms were constructed by a mothership company whereby a large range of competing funds could be purchased through one site (by telephone, before internet). Sector funds were created that focused on Europe, Asia, technology, and gold. All of the mutual funds fixed their "net asset value" (the price of the fund) at the close of the day based on the closing price of the component parts.

"Plime', you are a wise young man, but you are a financial novice. As a seasoned academician, you know you need a better database. You should quantify the correlation but the strongest correlation does not establish causality. However, you have to start somewhere, and I think you're on a good trail. Keep sniffing. Be your own devil's advocate."

"Feter Sol, thanks for your direction. I agree that more work is needed. I plan to start by creating some graphs to demonstrate the relationship of gold to fund pricing."

"Plime', you're describing a classic 'black box' approach to a 'white box' problem. You would be much better off if you convert this to a 'white box' inquiry." (In a black box approach, one sees what goes into the black box on one side and what comes out the other side. With a white box approach, one looks into the box to see the mechanisms – the cogs and levers – that cause the changes.) "Graphs will be a good starting point to define buy signals, but you need to study exit points as carefully as you study your entries. In trading, 50% of the effort goes to buying and 80% goes to selling." Uncle Sol continued, "I admire computer skills, but they are just a supplement to common sense. If you make twenty cents per trade, you can trade forever. Once you lose your chips, you are out of the game. Do your homework before you go real time with real money."

"Thank you, Sir. I will work on this. Good luck on your cotton trade."

"Plime', don't let this gold game interfere with your surgical career. Remember, the main thing should remain the main thing. To have real fulfillment in life, you must be a servant. You must first serve your God, then your family, and then your business. This numbers game that you are entertaining is after that. It is just a game. If you go down this golden rabbit trail, recognize it as a peripheral hobby. The balance sheet of your life is more than a set of numbers."

"Thanks, Feter Sol."

Defining the Black Box of the Gold Trade

I accepted the challenge from Uncle Solomon. Here was the setting; November, 1986. Young surgeon. Wife with two boys. Early in career. Time was/is a priority. Wife had business trip to New York City – my opportunity to join her with a few days away from my practice. Best Western Hotel, two or three blocks off Broadway. Quite posh by Tippah standards. Third-floor room. Plan: do the numbers; hard numbers; no bias; define the black box. The inputs for study were the closing prices of gold futures; the output was the gold mutual fund price.

XY graphs confirmed an unequivocal one-day lag between the closing price of gold and the gold mutual fund. Correlation coefficients were not necessary as the graphs were obvious. The stale pricing with a one-day lag was also confirmed in only one of 10 gold mutual funds that were analyzed. A model of "if-then" formulas was generated on an Excel platform; the optimized entry (purchase) was a two dollar increase in gold and the exit was determined to be any decrease. The study period was only three months. Real time trading of the inefficient price appeared justified. As a caveat, causality was never established; the reason for the lag and "stale" pricing was never clear. Secondly, no systemic crises occurred during the study period.

Putting the System to Work

"Feter Sol, Plimenik here!" I said on the phone. "It is real. I have confirmed the pricing inefficiency for the 3-month –"

He interrupted me. "Just a minute, Plime'…" His muffled voice followed: "Cover those shorts. Market price. Let's end our pain." He then returned to me. "Sorry Plime', better to lose a small skirmish than a major battle. The boys in New York got me on that trade. What's up?" In many previous conversations, he had explained the necessity of separating emotions from winning or losing but, to that point, he had failed miserably.

"Feter, the lag is real. At least, it was real for the studied time. I only had $8000 but I did my first trade with a 1.5% return on the first day. One phone call got me in; another got me out the next day. No hiccups. I want to add leverage." I paused hoping for his input – and hopefully financial support – but heard nothing. I was not surprised in view of his morning trading loss. "I'm going to my local banker and try to juice this up."

"Okay, Plime', borrow some seed money and come to me when you want to plant a full crop, after you establish some kind of track record." He cleared his throat with his unique guttural sound, a heralding sound of an impending Feter Sol soliloquy, "I have always enjoyed your display of youthful enthusiasm. Reminds me of myself in earlier days. I urge you, be cautious. Leverage cuts both ways. With any streak of bad luck, the borrower can become a slave to the lender. Trading is a loner business, so don't expect someone to catch you if you fall. And somewhere… somewhere, there will be someone who wants you to fall. There are so many traps in life. Of course, unpredictable systemic traps could affect your trading, but traps of priority affect your very life. I continue to suffer from bad decisions made in my earlier life over what were, in retrospect, trifling matters. Remember: God, family, business. I know your heart is good. Stay focused."

"Thanks, Uncle Sol."

A few days later, I received an envelope from Feter Sol. Two pages. Three-hole punched. Same format as twenty years earlier.

On page one, another copy of the hand-written note from twenty years previous:

#5 GOD, Family, business, games
…and in that order
Feter Sol, July 4, 1967

On page two:

#6 How much better to get wisdom than gold,
To choose understanding rather than silver!
The crucible for silver and the furnace for gold,
But the Lord tests the heart.
Mishlei 16:17; 17:3

Leverage

Next day. Afternoon appointment with local banker who had helped with my home mortgage several years earlier.

"Mr. Lee, I would like to borrow some money to fund a gold trading system that I have discovered." Mr. Lee leaned back in his chair and his eyes rolled upwards in a manner that we would call "walled back" in the South. I then went on to explain the pricing discrepancy in what seemed like an opportunity for safe speculation. My request was to borrow $50,000; I would add my $8000 (net $58k). I agreed to stop the program if the net balance dropped to $54,000, thus offering safety for the bank.

"But Doc, if you are trading this every day, we have no fixed collateral on the loan." Lowering his glasses, he leaned back in his chair showing a glimpse of almost fatherly reflection. "I really like you and I know you are good for $50,000, but be careful. I don't question your ability, but you are wandering into a ferocious battlefield."

"Thank you, Mr. Lee. Yes, I will be careful. Oh, one other thing. When I make 10%, I would like to borrow $50,000 again," I said with a careful smile.

It took one month and one day to make 10%. Next, Mr. Lee agreed to the second $50,000. I tested the waters a bit and told him that I would like to borrow $100,000 next time. In the next six weeks, we made another 10% gain. The $100,000 request was not granted: too much risk for a non-collateralized loan. The very next week, the president of the other bank (Jackson was basically a two-bank city at the time) came to the hospital with an acute surgical illness. After I performed an emergency laparotomy, he did very well and recovered without complication. On the day of his discharge, I told him of my gold venture and took the opportunity to inquire about additional funding. I'll never forget his response: "Doc, how much do you want and when do you want it?"

After two successful quarters, I reported back to Uncle Solomon. He added additional funds and agreed to assume primary responsibility for making the daily trades. I monitored the progress and continued research. Still, it was personally most gratifying to call my uncle every day after a substantial gain. We shared the euphoria of a "good lick" (residual Tippah terminology). Whenever I dialed his number, I recalled his admonition under the Tippah County red oak tree: "Good business is based on math and science and then psychology... There are always opportunities."

***

Uncle Sol was correct in warning me about systemic risk. Black Monday. October 19, 1987. Due to the panic with so many investors calling the parent company and, perhaps, brokers refusing to answer, Uncle Solomon could not make phone contact to exit our positions. We sustained a major hit. The setback was made up within 30 days. IT WAS A GOOD YEAR. The original account returned 122% in the first twelve months; the second and third accounts returned 99% and 92%.

But the Lord tests the heart...

5 GOD, GOLD AND JEWS

March, 1988.
37 years old.
16 months into "investing."

While Feter Sol reaped the harvest from the inefficiency of the new gold fund, I enjoyed discussing the venture with close friends, some of whom became joint investors. One of my friends, a Jewish economics professor, argued that my system was just a modern version of centuries-old arbitrage.

"Two hundred years ago, the English profited from the price difference between gold and silver in London versus India," he said. "The problem then was the risk and fear of the sailing time over the course of the year. You have reduced your 'sailing time' to less than 24 hours."

He asked about the logistics of trading in that I had a full-time surgical practice. I explained that the system required only one decision a day and my uncle was primarily responsible for implementing the trades.

"Who is your uncle?" he asked.

"He is probably the leading cotton trader in Memphis. You might know his family. They are also Jewish."

"You must be talking about Solomon Goldfarb."

He then proceeded to discuss the prominence of Jews in the world's financial history. He followed with another challenging question: WHY? Why have Jews been so prominent in finance? Which is more important: Jewish ethnicity or Jewish religion? Can they be separated? I responded that I had no clue. However, I knew my next step was obvious: consult with my Uncle Solomon.

***

Phone call the next morning.

"Feter Sol, Plimenik here! I hope I caught you on the right side of your trade this morning."

"Plime', yes, I'm on the right side of a cotton trade for now. However, I was about to call you. I have something more important to tell you." His bubbly exuberance exceeded that of a profitable trade.

"Goldfarb has a superstar guest coming from Alexandria – that's Alexandria of Egypt – and by way of Paris. I will fill you in later, but I am planning a dinner and would like for you and your wife to come. I will have several people from Goldfarb here. Should I invite Wilbur and Maxine?" he asked in a near manic phase and then promptly answered, "Of course, no. But you called me this morning. What's on your mind?"

"Feter Sol, you are too excited! Alexandria? Tell me more."

"Plime', no more clues. I want you to be here in person. It's my surprise. Now, can you come the first Saturday night in April?"

"Of course. This is distinctly unusual for you, and I would not miss it."

"Great! Now what is your question for this morning?" asked Uncle Solomon.

"Feter Sol, I had dinner with one of our clients last night. He is an economics professor in town. He challenged me with a question about why the Jews have been so dominant in world finance. I'll bet you have an opinion. Do you have time to share it?"

"My dear Plimenik, I have all the time in the world for you. Now be specific with me. What question would you like to address?"

"The question relates to the possible interplay between Jewish ethnicity, faith and finance. I have been quick to tell my economics professor that my favorite uncle and closest mentor happens to be Jewish. And, who knows, my own ancestry might also be traced back to the Ten Lost Tribes from Ancient Israel. My pet theory is hard to prove, but one of the Ten Lost Tribes may have settled in Wales, my paternal area of origin. But back to the question, why have Jews been so dominant in finance?"

"Plimenik, Jews have been dominant in many academic fields besides finance – not just today – but throughout Western civilization. We have been recognized in medicine, law, and science. You may be surprised to know how many Nobel Prize winners and chess champions are Jewish. But, our dominance in finance has impacted world trade..." He paused, "I trust you have time for a mini-lecture."

"Of course, that's what I expected," I answered.

"Well to begin, usury -- or lending money for interest, regardless of the rate – was frowned upon in the earliest literature of Jews, Christians, and Muslims..."

A Feter Sol soliloquy followed.

(If history is of little interest to you, skip to non-italicized.)

"The time value of money as a concept was not blessed in ancient bartering economies. However, Jews were allowed to loan money for interest to non-Jewish people, and they became accepted moneylenders for wealthy Muslims and Christians. When the Christians tried to reclaim Jerusalem in the Crusades, the Church forbad trade with the Muslims. The Europeans still wanted the peppers, the spices and the silks from the East; Jews again filled the gap and became middlemen with the Arab trade. The Jews may have been derided as opportunists and scavengers of commerce, but they fulfilled a need for the majority population.

"Then came the Italian Renaissance in the 1400s. Most of the books state the Renaissance claim a 'rebirth' of Greco-Roman art and literature. That's the romantic answer. My perspective may sound crude but the arts flourished only after the Christians began to make extra money; they exploited the tools of usury. With money came art; whenever there is no money, there is no art. The Church – ostensibly opposed to any form of money lending – became a major beneficiary as the bankers offered gifts of art to the Church to atone for their capitalist sins. The Medici family of Florence founded the first truly international bank; for his contributions, Lorenzo de Medici has been labelled the Godfather of the Renaissance. Of course, the banks could not have functioned had it not been for the adoption of the Arabic numbering system… which would not have been possible without the Jewish trading with the Arabs. The Arabic numbering system provided the numeric language for calculating interest, bookkeeping, and banking. Once the Arabic numbering system was recognized, the abacus and Roman numerals were antiquated (except for numbering up aristocracy and Super Bowls).

"The Jews probably would have introduced earlier banking had it not been for the Christian laws. You see, Jewish money lending in Florence was limited to pawn lending. You will find this interesting: in the Old Market, their pawn stations were marked by a red badge or red shield. That's an important symbol. Many Jews migrated to northern Europe where they created an even more elaborate and sophisticated bank. You know

35

their name – the Rothschild family. By the way, they marked the first bank in
Frankfurt with an important symbol. You might guess it! It was a red shield. You know
that 'red shield' in German is 'Rothschild.' The Rothschild banking conglomerate
continues to have a major international influence. Their cultural descendants in America
created the firm of Goldman Sachs. Even more astounding is their continued influence
through the world's central banks and even the Federal Reserve."

"Feter Sol, I appreciate your nice synopsis, but my question is more difficult. Is there a variance of cultural norms that led to the Jews being more successful? If so, what is the basis for the variance?"

"Plimenik, you pose difficult questions. Remember, strong correlations don't establish causality. Of course, socio-biologic factors might theoretically lead to higher IQ scores in one ethnic group, but the subject is considered too inflammatory for public discussion. Any attempt to designate cultural norms is often declared as shameful stereotyping. Along that line of thinking, some have even suggested that the Jewish faith 'emphasizes pursuits in this world as opposed to the afterlife.'[4] Perhaps you might do a forensic comparison of Jewish versus Christian literature. See what an academic can conclude."

"Forensic comparison? What do you mean?"

"Direct your investigation to compare the respective literature of both Jewish and Christian groups. The Jewish literature is called the Scripture. Christians refer to Scripture as the Old Testament; of course, the Christian literature recognizes the Old Testament as prophecy fulfilled in the New Testament. The first five books of the Scripture are collectively called The Law or The Torah. Skeptics may argue about modern application, but they can't argue about consistency over time. Our Jewish Scripture remains unchanged for at least 2200 years as authenticated by the Dead Sea Scrolls. Start with your black box approach for both the Old and New Testaments. Use simple inputs."

"Simple inputs?" I asked.

"Yes, ask simple questions, such as the relative incidence of gold and silver in both sets of literature. Find the first reports of the precious metals. Look for any subtle or implied message, when applied over the

---

[4] Burnstein, Paul (2007). Jewish educational and economic success in the United States: a search for explanations. Sociological Perspectives, 50, 209-228.

centuries. Watch for any bias. Remember, correlations don't necessarily imply causality."

"Thanks, Feter Sol."

***

I completed the study.

1) "Gold" occurred 10 times more frequently in the Old versus New Testament (377 vs. 36, NIV); "silver" occurred 17 times more frequently (288 vs. 16, NIV). Although the Old Testament is twice as long as the New, the differences are real. The precious metals received more emphasis on a numerical basis in the Old versus the New Testament. The difference might be/could be significant.

2) The first "gold" was found surprisingly early in the Scripture. (See Genesis 2:10-12 NLT: "*A river flowed from the land of Eden... around the entire land of Havilah, where gold is found.*) Later in that chapter, Eve was created from one of Adam's ribs. Note that gold was introduced prior to Eve; is this significant?

3) The first "silver" was also found early in the Scripture. In three virtually identical anecdotes, a family patriarch disingenuously declared that his wife was not his wife, but instead a sister, to avoid being slain by the pharaoh/king. Subsequently, the family patriarch amassed considerable wealth, silver, and gold (from Genesis 13:2, 20:16, 26:9-14). What lesson of negotiating ethics is implied by these three anecdotes?

4) The New Testament places a lower value on earthly wealth compared to the Old Testament.

I surmised that the lasting prominent literature of any ethnic group should either contribute to or be reflected in cultural norms. In logical extension of forensic review, the early Scripture may have contributed to the foundation and proclivity for Jewish achievements in many fields and, in particular, finance. After I accumulated the information, I reported to Uncle Solomon. I will never forget his response.

"Plime', your Feter Sol sent you on a Tippah County snipe hunt. You anticipated a catch of clarity. But, look! You are holding a bag of disconnected twigs and leaves. You should recognize that your comparative study reflects your bias in extrapolation. The two batches of history's great literature feature different times, different governments, and different maturity of ethnic groups. You cannot make conclusions based on what amount to historical controls at best. Once again, correlations do not establish causality. Not to worry, humanity has made the same error of logic for centuries. You're not alone."

Once again, Uncle Solomon had used Socratic methods to make his point and, in so doing, taught me a lesson about myself!

"And Plime', I look forward to seeing you after the sun sets this Saturday." Then he paused. "It's our Hebrew tradition to celebrate at the conclusion of Shabbat. This will be a celebration... a celebration, indeed."

6 THE FRENCH-EGYPTIAN JEWESS

Saturday night dinner.
Uncle Solomon's home.
April, 1988.
My age: 38 years.

Three-story Victorian mansion in East Memphis. Columns; more columns. I admired the elaborate glasswork on the front door which featured an etched name "HAVILAH." As we entered the grand atrium, we were offered a champagne flute by a tuxedo-clad English butler.

"Doctor and Mrs. Voyles, I'm so pleased that you arrived early. Mr. Goldfarb has hors-d'oeuvres in his library. He also wishes to tease your intellect with his wisterian challenge."

We were directed into the regal room. Dark mahogany furniture. Ornate lamps – French baroque. Carpet chosen by Uncle Solomon in Istanbul. I was immediately impressed by the scent of fresh cut flowers. Two ornate Victorian era vases were the focal point of the room. Each contained a separate variety of flowering wisteria. I was comparing the two when Uncle Solomon entered the room.

"Ah, Pleminik! I see you are entranced by my wisterian puzzle. These two plants hold a clue to botanical evolution. Let me show you–"

"Sol, my dear friend!" We were abruptly interrupted by the boisterous entry of Harvey Walton, the president of the Memphis Cotton Exchange. "We're so excited! Who is this surprise guest that we are going to meet?"

"Harvey! I told you this is a surprise. My special guest will be introduced only when all of the other guests are here. In the meantime, study my two wisteria plants. They hold a hidden answer regarding evolution..."

In short order, other guests filed in. For the men, the uniform of the day was standard: three-piece suits; colorful ties; two-toned wingtips. For the women, exquisite dresses... likely Goldfarb products. When it was apparent that all were present, Uncle Solomon took a position in the pillared atrium about a third of the way up a spiral staircase. He tapped his champagne glass. With a nod to his English butler, the room was filled with background music of Elvis. *Are you lonesome tonight? Do you miss me tonight? Are you sorry we drifted apart...*

The volume was turned down as rehearsed, and Solomon began his introduction. "Ladies and gentlemen, today is a unique day for the city of Memphis..." He took a signature pause, raised his left eyebrow and cleared his throat. "On this day, we are all truly blessed to have in our company a European princess who is on a tour of American music. The princess has become my dear friend. As you will see shortly, she represents the ultimate embodiment of glamour. You ladies were invited as you obviously appreciate glamour. You men were invited as an afterthought." There was an obligatory chuckle with Solomon's attempt at humor. "Our guest was born in Paris, but her ethnic roots tie her to the grand city of Alexandria, Egypt. She is a beautiful amalgamation of all the wonders of the Mediterranean. She has reached the absolute pinnacle in the glamour world – first in Paris and then in the United States. What you don't know is this: I first met this dazzling young lady in Paris at one of my lectures when she was first pursuing her graduate studies. I have watched her grow. I now watch her glow. I am blessed to be her friend. I present to you... Coco."

On cue, Elvis resumed. *Does your memory stray to a bright sunny day when I kissed you and called you sweetheart?* All eyes were drawn to the top of the stairs. Like the Egyptian sphinx rising in the distance, the Alexandrian princess slowly emerged. Coco. *The Coco*. She floated across the balcony, commanding the attention of all. *Tell me, dear, are you lonesome tonight?* We were her prey, captured by her elegance. Or, was it exotic charm, her luxurious olive-colored skin, or those unique emerald eyes? She began the descent of the stairs. Her hair bounced on her shoulders and amplified a mammary jiggle. Then legs. All legs. More legs. Her giraffe extensions were exaggerated by her spike heels but even more so by the cling of her skirt. *Who else imagined her as a gyrating belly dancer of the Middle East? Was I the only one to notice the lateral slit that framed the muscular pulses of her left thigh?*

My critical analysis was suddenly interrupted by a sharply pointed elbow to my rib section from my wife. And then, across the room... *CRASH!* President Walton dropped his champagne glass. It shattered. The English butler scurried in response. The men stared; the women glared. Uncle Solomon smiled. Coco tipped her head. And with her French accent, she purred, "Good evening. As you are friends of my dear Solomon, you are friends of Coco."

Coco enjoyed her practiced display of youthful splendor. Resuming her descent, she stopped a step below Uncle Solomon and smiled at her audience. That's when I first noticed the dazzling sparkle of a walnut-sized ruby adorning her navel. Embracing my uncle, she planted a kiss to each cheek and proclaimed with a sensuous French accent, "I love you, Sol." As if on cue, the decades-older ladies spontaneously and collectively displayed an artful facial mosaic... but the theme would be repugnance. Elvis whined. *Tell me dear, are you lonesome tonight...*

***

Uncle Solomon's relationship with Coco's family began in the late 1940s with the trade of Egyptian cotton in Alexandria. Fleeing the ultraconservative Muslim movement, the Egyptian cotton broker moved his family to Paris. Uncle Solomon's cousin, Fritz, assisted them in their immigration. Coco was born in Paris in 1965. Like many families from Alexandria, Coco's family tree was a bit variegated or perhaps best described as bouillabaisse. Her father was ostensibly a Coptic Christian with roots to Syria. Her mother was of Jewish ancestry with a long-term presence in Alexandria.

In his business trips to Paris, Solomon became smitten by the young daughter of his old broker friend. Although she was quite stunning, the young lady was struggling as a model in the highly competitive Parisian market. Uncle Solomon came to her aid with the assistance of Fritz, an established stalwart in high-end fashion. With their combined joint support, Coco advanced quickly to stardom. One other thing: her real name was Abishag Shunami. Her professional name chosen by Uncle Solomon: Coco!

Solomon spared no expense in supporting his Coco. Lavish Parisian essentials were patterned after Coco Chanel. Together, they visited the famous coffee shop known as Angelina on rue Rivoli where Chanel had had her daily chocolate. As proclaimed by management, "Angelina is a tranquil, exquisite space, somewhere between serenity and indulgence," certainly an appropriate locale for an early and rapid transition to elegance in the fashion industry. Coco's well-furnished flat was located on the Right Bank just beyond Pont Neuf, but on frequent occasions, she and Uncle Solomon celebrated at Coco Chanel's final residence: the Ritz at Place Vendome. Of course, Coco was provided with personal trainers and coaching professionals. She quickly adjusted to her new life style. It is no wonder that she had such admiration for her faithful friend... my uncle... my Feter Sol. Even when she reached celebrity status, she remained forever loyal.

Success in Paris led to success in the American market. Coco had photo appearances in New York and Los Angeles. Yes, Uncle Solomon was her senior travel companion pictured in the celebrity news. Typical for the French, Coco enjoyed American music. In particular, she was fascinated with Elvis Presley. It was no surprise when she asked Uncle Solomon to take her to Graceland, the museum of the late Elvis. That request is what brought Coco to Memphis. A private tour: the "tour d'Elvis." It was a glaring weakness of my uncle that he always embellished his successes and he was no less reluctant to show off his glamour princess.

After the introduction, cocktails and champagne were followed by a multicourse gourmet dinner. President Walton was seated next to Coco and spent the evening enthralled by Uncle Solomon's new friend. As the wine flowed, a series of toasts was inevitable.

President Walton, forever competing as alpha male was first to raise his glass. "As president of the Memphis Cotton Exchange, I am prone to deal with superlatives. That is in large part due to my association with super people. So first, I toast my friend Sol. He has earned the superlative for he is the master of the cotton trade."

"Hear, hear! To the master of the cotton trade," echoed the guests.

"More importantly, I raise my glass to toast his new friend Coco. From my perspective, there has never been a better setting more appropriate for introducing this sparkle of French-Egyptian splendor..." He paused and surveyed the room. "One thing for certain, no jeweler could create a more perfect setting for that gorgeous red ruby."

"Harvey! Sit down!" scolded Mrs. Walton.

"Just a word or two more, Dear." He resumed his toast. "To the beautiful young lady who has blessed us with her presence, we stand in awe... and I might say envy," as he winked at Solomon. "We raise our glass to Coco."

"Hear, hear. Coco... Coco..." echoed the crowd.

Far too many toasts followed. It was time for the evening to end. Feter Sol looked to me with his signature raised eyebrow, which I took as my cue to complete the evening.

"I raise my glass to the man whom I greatly admire. To you, he may be known as the master of the cotton trade, but to me he is a dear uncle who has been my mentor from youth. I offer a closing toast to my Feter Sol. Let's enjoy the peace of the evening. Shalom."

In a hearty response, "Shalom!"

As a departing gesture, President Walton whispered in Solomon's ear "For one night, I would like to trade places with Absalom on your rooftop. Absalom! Oh, Absalom!" *Who is Absalom?*[5]

***

After the tour of Graceland, Coco insisted on a day trip to the birthplace of Elvis in Tupelo, Mississippi. To round out her sample of the culture of rural northeast Mississippi, Solomon offered to take her to Pine Hill to visit the grave site of my Aunt Grace. That's when she also suggested that she would like to visit my home place near Falkner. I knew it was not a good idea but Solomon, forever mesmerized by his young princess, was insistent in satisfying all her requests.

Solomon had decided that he would introduce Coco to Tippah as the graduate student from Paris. Unfortunately, Coco's wardrobe did not include "rural Tippah" nor did she appreciate the conservative attitude that she was about to encounter. From the instant that those long legs protruded out the door of Solomon's new Mercedes, it became obvious to Solomon that he had made a major mistake. Although it was a muggy day,

---

[5] According to the account from Scripture, King David had a son named Absalom who attempted to overthrow the kingdom of his father. Absalom was almost successful in the insurrection and he did temporarily take control of Jerusalem. As a show of disdain for his father, he had sexual relationships with several of King David's concubines in public view on the roof of his Palace (2 Samuel 16:22).

the air in the big house iced. No welcoming greeting. The women scattered like a disrupted ant hill before retreating to the kitchen.

"Solomon! How could you?" said Aunt Maxine as she departed. "Some graduate student you say…. I never trusted you anyway. You are despicable. And to think, you just went to Grace's grave. You can get back in your Mercedes with your girlie friend and go back to Memphis."

Solomon recognized the futility of compromise and escorted Coco back to the car. They made a hasty departure. His last visit to the home place.

***

"That Hebrew rascal! We should have never trusted him," said Aunt Maxine as she returned to the family conference room… that would be the kitchen.

"She's a woman of the night!"

"A harlot!"

"I'll bet Solomon picked her up on one of them high-end streets in Paris…"

"Sister, now she's his concubine."

"Shame on all of y'all," I continued. "You women are just jealous and you men are just full of envy. As I said, shame on y'all…."

"Well, just because you made a surgeon don't mean you know anything at all about right and wrong – especially for Tippah County…"

"And to think, she dressed like that knowing there would be kids here," continued Aunt Maxine. "I can't get over it. All 'nipped out' in that see-through blouse. All those jewels on her necklace dangling between those little 'pointy-outy' breasts. You would have thought she would have the decency to wear something like we wear. Sisters, there ain't nothing wrong with calico."

"Another thing, she probably is a Muslim," cried out a raspy voice of an uncle.

"I am so disappointed in Solomon…"

"Now we know why he spent so much time in Paris…"

"He has disgraced us all bringing such foreign filth to Tippah County…"

"And think of sweet Grace. I am sure that she is rolling over in her grave up at Pine Hill."

"All the while, that wretched Solomon is carousing in his Egyptian bed sheets…"

"No wonder he got so excited when he talked about 500 thread count. Them sheets are a sign of sin! We will burn our sheets before the sun goes down," said Uncle Wilbur.

"Not so fast, Wilbur," said Aunt Maxine. "You ain't gonna burn my sheets…"

And then there was a moment of quiet as all of my aunts and uncles took a breath before repeating the chorus, just like at the a cappella choir: "She's Solomon's concubine… No, she's a harlot… No, she's a gol-durned French whore."

7 KUALA LUMPUR

Looking back, 1986-88 were defining years in so many ways. First, the gold experiment paid off handsomely. Unfortunately, the Coco disaster in Tippah marked a turning point in family relations; Uncle Solomon vowed that he would die before visiting Tippah again. By contrast, my fondness for my uncle – starting in the days of hand-cranked ice cream – only grew stronger. Still I would wonder about my uncle's judgment with his Tippah introduction of Coco: *Feter Sol, what were you thinking? What did you expect? Given any audience, the scantily clad Coco would by nature resort to her catwalk stride: a perfected look-at-me rhumba. Yes, it works in Paris. No, not in rural Tippah. Your counsel has always seemed so wise… except for yourself.*

Oh, one final thing: the spring of 1988 brought the end of the gold trade. Uncle Sol was attending a finance conference in Paris, and I had the responsibility for managing the gold trade. Here's the actual conversation.

***

May, 1988

"Yes, I would like to move my entire balance from cash to the gold fund," I said to a pleasant female voice from 1-800 land. There was momentary silence.

"Excuse me sir, but are you aware of the new regulations?" asked the lady.

"No, I'm unaware of any change. What's new?"

"Sir, we initially set up our fund trading rules with no limits on the frequency of exchanges into or out of our funds. Also, we charged no fees any transactions. Both policies were designed to encourage investors to put their money in our funds. It worked. A few investors – we call them *market-timers* -- traded in and out of the fund very frequently, and we are trying to curtail their activity. We have three major changes. First of all, we will limit each client to four exchanges per year. Second, we mandate a two-month holding period. Third, we will impose a 2% redemption fee on any earlier withdrawals."

"Let me think about it. I may call you back." *Market-timer? What a nasty intonation she used! Might as well have called me a child molester.*

It was over! After a wonderful ride of eighteen months, the gold trade was over. The inefficiency of "newness" had been corrected. No more extraordinary returns! The bush-whacking path of the pioneer had given way to established routes with paved roads, speed limits and red lights. Uncle Sol had been right: unpredictable inefficiencies tend to occur with any new investment products, but they will be corrected by market forces.

***

"Feter Sol, it's over," I said with an immediate phone call to my uncle in Paris.

"What's over, Plime'?"

"The gold trade. It's over. The fund has implemented trading limitations with punitive redemption fees on short-term trades. It's over."

"Plimenik, no system works forever. Thanks to your eagle eye and Myron Kandel back in '86, you identified an inefficiency as it sprouted in a developing market. My bet is that you were among the first to exploit the inefficiency. But now, it has been corrected. It's the same way with every new edge in markets. They are time-limited. By the way, I met the manager of your fund at the gold conference here in Paris. He gave me a prospectus of his gold fund. I read it this morning. Do you know where their management is?"

"I assume it's in New York or Philadelphia with the parent company. Am I wrong?" I asked.

"Yes, you're wrong," said Uncle Sol. "The management is in London... London, Plime'. And London played a critical role in your gold trade."

"I don't understand. What do you mean?"

"Plime', the parent American fund company – in haste to get a gold sector fund in a new emerging business – partnered with an existing gold fund manager from London. On reviewing their portfolio, about 65% of the mining companies of the 'American' gold fund are located in countries of the previous Royal Empire: South Africa and Australia. Critically, those mining company stocks are traded only in London, not traded in New York. Accordingly, the

London-based stocks have their price fixed on the London afternoon close. Since afternoon London occurs at mid-morning New York, the daily net asset value in New York is based on a several-hour 'stale' London price. Several of the Australian stocks were priced even earlier. Thus, the fund is effectively and predictably mispriced, virtually every day. That's why your gold trading system worked so well. Plime', you know this: *understanding causality always trumps correlation.*"

I thought a minute. I could almost smell cherry tobacco from across the Atlantic. Uncle Solomon was a clever man. He loved riddles, particularly financial ones. In this case, he had solved the riddle of the black box. He saw the cogs and levers that made the black box work. The black box was now a white box. Stock prices were fixed at local closing times around the globe, but U.S. mutual funds apply that price at the New York close without adjusting for the interval change. The afternoon closing price in London occurred at mid-morning in the U.S. Any additional rise in the gold price in our afternoon would not be reflected in the London-based mining stocks until the next day.

"Dear Feter, you are a genius. You opened the black box and saw the levers. I feel like the novice that I am. I should have figured this out a long time ago."

"But Plime', perhaps my stronger Hebrew heritage gave me an advantage," he chuckled. "Your biblical studies suggest that we Jewish peddlers have a more established history in recognizing trade opportunities. Problems always create opportunity. Remember the Rothschilds and the Lehman brothers. We have been figuring out financial puzzles for centuries."

[The Rothschilds offset financial risk by lending to both sides in European wars. The Lehman Brothers - or their cousins – reportedly executed similar strategies in the United States Civil War by blockade-running and delivering cotton to New England for a 5-to-1 profit. The Jewish businessmen were called 'opportunists' and 'scavengers of commerce.' Gen. U.S. Grant issued a proclamation (Edict 11) whereby all Jews would be expelled from Kentucky, Tennessee and Mississippi. Of course, President Lincoln quickly rescinded the proclamation.]

"Feter Sol, why am I not surprised to receive another history lesson? Your Hebrew ancestors just cracked another set of black boxes and were clever enough to exploit them."

"Your golden observation was also very clever," Uncle Solomon added. "The initial rules of the frontier were too lax. We exploited the flaw. At some point, the gains from unlimited transactions were no longer offset by increased assets. Somewhere, a manager labelled you as a 'scavenger of commerce.'" Again, he paused for a self-gratifying chuckle. "The glorified gold peddler won the first round with market timing. Industry then refined their rules. Your gold game ended. That's capitalism."

"Is there anything wrong with market timing?" I asked.

"Oh no, there's nothing wrong or illegal about market timing. Besides, we just made the phone calls; the fund made the actual trades. Despite the altruistic claims on TV commercials, the mutual fund industry is driven by *their* profit, not yours. They do not measure progress with merit badges like the Boy Scouts."

"That makes sense," I said.

"Plime', I would argue that everyone is a market timer. It's just a matter of holding period. Some people hold until their death, at which time their children liquidate their assets. Some hold until their retirement, some hold until next week, and some hold for a few hours. Who knows? Someday, there may be a trade based on nanoseconds. There is nothing intrinsically wrong with trying to time the markets, but the effort is usually futile. Now that they have changed the rules, you will have to adjust. It's a cat-and-mouse proposition. Now let me ask you a penetrating question: do you really think it's still over?"

"Well, I assume it's over," I said.

"No, dear Plime', it's not over. There are always opportunities… opportunities that might yield more gold than the gold fund. Think with me. Ignore the black box. Think white box."

He paused long enough to give me time to ponder but his riddle escaped me. I could sense that he was puffing on his pipe and enjoying his challenge. Socrates would have been proud. When I failed to answer, he made an even more perplexing statement: "Plime', are you still there? Allow me to point you in another direction…. Think Kuala Lumpur."

"I appreciate the message of white box, but I don't have a clue about Kuala Lumpur and what it means. I don't think I could find it on a map," I said.

"Plime', try again. Think white box. Hear me? And then, think Kuala Lumpur. Orient your mind to white box and think Southeast Asia… uh, shall I say 'orient to the Orient,'" he said, giving me ample time to think. "Think like a scavenger of commerce."

"The answer to your riddle is not obvious." I could sense his smile from across the Atlantic. "Offer me some more direction."

"Re-look at the levers that made your gold trade work. Then, think Kuala Lumpur," he repeated. "Next, you might think Jakarta. Then, Singapore. Same applies to Hong Kong."

"Feter, they are all major cities in Southeast Asia. Am I getting warmer? Tell me more," I said.

"We have a worldwide rally in new tech stocks. Many of the components are built in emerging markets of Southeast Asia. Their countries are witnessing major expansion and the volatile Asian stocks are in rally mode. But, Asian markets trade while we sleep. Their prices are fixed before the sun rises over New York. As a scavenger of commerce, I have this sneaky suspicion that price action in the emerging markets mirrors the action of the United States on the previous day. A black box study of correlates will confirm my suspicion. We can buy Southeast Asia mutual funds at the end of a good day on the US markets and go to bed anticipating a happy return after a good night's sleep."

"I've got it! Causality trumps correlation. White box trumps black box. Same form of arbitrage, same technique, different instruments. I've got it. Kuala Lumpur."

Uncle Sol continued. "Once you've opened the white box, you can see the cogs and levers. There's a bigger rabbit on the trail."

"Feter, the human brain is amazing. I just had a flashback of a ruby red Cadillac in my youth with a message that *'wisdom is more precious than rubies.'*"

"'Plime', this will be bigger than the gold market. Let's get together as soon as I get home from Paris. In the meantime, start analyzing why the gold trade ended so quickly. What precautions can we take to increase the longevity of a potential Asia trade? We must protect our partners in the mutual fund industry."

"Feter Sol, let's meet as soon as you get home. Maybe over the Memorial Day weekend. The markets will be closed. In the meantime, I will do some cursory investigations in preparation."

"There is something I have to tell you." He paused. "I came to Paris for a more important reason than the gold conference. Since my youth, this City of Light has been my personal oasis for in-depth introspection and decision making. Unknown to you, I have struggled with some major issues in the last decade. I have decided what I must do. I will make a major change in my life." There was a long pause. I thought we had been disconnected.

"Feter Sol, are you there?" I asked.

"Yes, Plime', I am still here. I don't know how to tell you this… I will soon be able to devote more time to the Asia trade." His voice cracked a bit with an unusual display of emotion. "I will be stepping down as president of Goldfarb Cotton."

"I don't understand. Why would you do that?" I asked.

"Did I ever tell you that polar bears eat their young?"

8 A WISTERIAN TWIST

Memorial Day, 1988.
Uncle Sol's home. Backyard veranda. White wicker furniture. Lavender table cloth.
Manicured lawn. Hydrangeas and wisteria in full bloom, also lavender. Ceiling fans
quietly spinning. Iced tea; of course, sweet tea.

"But Feter Sol, why in the world would you step down as president of
your company? You founded Goldfarb. You have been the strongest voice
of the Memphis Cotton Exchange. What is it that I don't know?" I asked.

He did not answer immediately. Rather, he seemed to be mesmerized
by the coalescing drops of water forming on the surface of the iced tea
glass. The drops trickled down to the white linen napkin with a lavender
monogram of *Havilah*.

"Plimenik, I am over 60 years old. It's time for some new direction."
He lit his pipe and leaned back in his chair. As Goldfarb Cotton had been
his life, he knew that I found his explanation incomplete. He was holding
back. "That's my story for the *Memphian Press*. It will not surprise you; there
is more to the story."

He took a deep breath and sighed in capitulation.

"I can't get the dominos to stop falling."

"Feter Sol, I don't understand. What was the first domino?" I asked.

"I'm afraid that you will be disappointed in your uncle. Remember
what Faulkner said: 'if a man doesn't admit to being ashamed of himself
now and then, he's not being honest.' Well, I admit to some shame but I
also declare honesty." He took a puff from his pipe, obviously choosing his

words as if pre-planned. "It began in the heyday of Goldfarb Cotton. Back in the sixties, trading cotton was a highly polished art form. Long-term trends in pricing were set by market fundamentals but the daily action was set by a handful of my strong friends spread across the cotton belt. We loved volatility... even created it. My peddler background served me well. Opportunities were tremendous for the skilled hand," said Uncle Solomon. He paused.

"Your skill, I understand; your decision, I don't."

"Plime', one of my trading techniques was based on exploiting the weakness of novice speculators... amateurs from across the country... even amateurs in my own office."

I looked at him inquisitively. "Tell me more. I still don't understand."

"Do you remember the story about the young trader named Kruger?"

"Of course, I remember him. Strangely enough, I remember his real name: Joab," I said.

"You might remember that he lost a lot of money when he shorted cotton?"

"I remember."

"Well, his misfortune was not a matter as simple as bad luck or faulty analysis. He was absolutely correct that cotton prices were weak. He was right in direction, but he didn't understand how the daily markets really worked. He needed an early lesson."

He paused again.

"And I assume you gave him the lesson," I said, encouraging him to continue.

"Yes... I waited until he had established a heavy position. Then, I called my trading cronies in Georgia and Texas. We playfully called ourselves the Cotton Cartel. We joined forces and artificially pushed up the price. Cotton sky-rocketed in thin trading that afternoon. We created what was called a short squeeze in our business. We destroyed his position." He took a sip of his tea. "The minute after I saw that he covered his short position, we promptly sold our longs and we went short. We made money both ways. Kruger got slaughtered. Funny thing is, he didn't know why. It's the same as in a card game: if you don't know who the sucker is, you're the sucker. Kruger was so vulnerable, just like an infant polar bear being devoured by its mother."

"What happened next?" I asked, prompting him to continue.

"Kruger figured out what happened several years later when we *initiated* another new bear cub. I explained to Kruger that every novice has to pay an initiation fee. It's a step of personal maturation in the business, just like at the poker table."

"That seems like a tough initiation," I said.

"That it was. But Plime', I have told you: *this ain't Sunday school.* Besides, I paid the same fee in my youth and accepted it as the rules of engagement. Young Kruger was different. He was not satisfied even when I showed him how I had handsomely reimbursed him through other trading gains of the company. He remained indignant."

"Again, as your loving mentee, I can understand Kruger's point of view."

"Well… there's more. The next Monday morning after we sacrificed that second bear cub, the Feds invaded my office and demanded copies of my trading records. On the same day, they had search warrants for the offices of my friends in the Cotton Cartel. The records confirmed our collaboration, but nothing that we did was illegal."

"Feter Sol, then I still don't get it. Back to the question, why would you step down now?"

"Again… there is more. The Feds continued to harass me and periodically invaded my office for two years. The only good thing about their investigation was that it was kept confidential. You might understand that the press would love to trash us as greedy cotton traders and bad press, even if not true, could destroy my reputation. Well, I obviously concluded that young Kruger had contacted the Feds, but he vehemently denied it. On questioning him more, he sheepishly admitted that he had shared our methods with my half-brother, Wicked. Wicked hated me even after all these years, and I knew he had no reservations about causing me pain. In addition, the Goldfarb clothing industry had fallen on hard times, and I suspect he was looking for a whistleblower award. However, after two years of misery, the Feds, at the insistence of my lawyer, issued us a letter declaring no discernible wrongdoing. All that aside, the trading rules of the 1960s were lax, and Congress changed the rules of the game with the Commodities Futures Trading Commission Act of 1974. It limited the effectiveness of the Cotton Cartel and cut into the profit margin of Goldfarb. In retrospect, I guess it was not a bad thing…"

"Feter Sol, I still don't understand why you would quit as president."

"Plime', I was relieved and thought that all with the Feds was resolved... resolved until I saw the headlines in the following Monday morning's paper: *Goldfarb Cotton under Federal Investigation*. Just at the time that I was cleared by the Feds, I was convicted by the press. Actually, everything that the paper printed was largely factual; it was just incomplete. A staff writer from the paper had called me for an interview in the week before the article. I don't give interviews about my business so I declined. Frankly, I smelled a rat."

"I can understand that," I said.

"When the paper came out, my world began to crumble. Three big clients cancelled their accounts that very morning. By the afternoon, my speaking engagement to the students at Western Tennessee University was cancelled... supposedly due to scheduling conflicts. My next call was from Sister Florentina who headed up the Build a Better Memphis campaign; the Catholic board asked permission to list my Platinum Sponsorship as anonymous. She finished the conversation with 'Solomon, I trust you understand. The Sisters appreciate your hard work, and our Lord knows your heart.'"

"Surely, you went to the press to correct their report."

"Yes, on Tuesday morning, I went to the editor's office and showed him the letter from the Feds stating no discernible wrongdoing. The paper defended their story as accurate. I then asked them to confirm my half-brother as the undisclosed source. They refused to identify him, but the damage was done. In a fit of rage, I tried to reach Wicked. For the first time in decades, I called his office as well as his home but I was told that he was unavailable. He was on a gambling junket in Las Vegas. I knew I shouldn't have tried to call Wicked. I cooled off and called my friend Ben."

"Who is Ben?"

"I'm sorry. Ben's full name is Benaiah Joseph. He has been a true confidant since my teenage years. You know, as you ascend the socio-economic ladder, your true friends and trusted confidants are harder to find. Ben is a criminal defense lawyer, but he has given me sage advice over the years. I explained the complete situation to him. He had also known Wicked since childhood. His closing remarks were typical: 'Let me review the options. I'll get back to you.'"

"Feter Sol, that must have occurred over a decade ago when I was in my residency. Why step down now?"

"I am getting to that but hear me out. That very night, Wicked disappeared. Vanished. Gone. No parting phone calls to his family. No notes. No nothing. His personal belongings were found in his hotel room in Vegas along with the residual of a greasy room-service cheeseburger. There were no signs of intruders or a struggle. The hotel surveillance camera showed him getting into a yellow cab with what appeared to be a hooker. From that point, there was no trace of him. Unfortunately, because of my foolish phone calls, I was implicated in his disappearance. His family's attorney convinced the prosecutors to convene a grand jury investigation, but they declined to indict as there was no evidence linking me to foul play other than my phone calls. Frankly, Ben found out that Wicked had huge gambling debts which were likely the reason for his demise. The Vegas mafia has a cruel way of collecting bad debts..."

"Feter Sol, I am sorry that you had to go through all that turmoil. I know it must have been tragic but that was also ten years ago. I never heard about any of it as I was away in my training. But still, why would you step down now? It seems to me that you successfully dealt with the accusations."

"Your neighborhood author wrote that in any battle, victory is an illusion of philosophers and fools. There was no victory. He also wrote that past is not dead..."

"It's not even past," I interrupted. "Feter Sol, what are you not telling me?"

"Plime', a body was unearthed this past month in Vegas. The skeletal remains look like they may be Wicked's. Bullet hole through the skull. The story has not made the Memphis press, but the Memphis FBI agent has already called me and instructed me not to leave Memphis again until this is settled. They are awaiting dental records. The agent made a flippant remark that it is too bad that Kruger's no longer around."

"What does that mean? Where is Kruger now?"

"Kruger is dead."

"Dead? What happened to him?"

"He was murdered in Chicago."

"How did that happen?" I asked.

57

"It's a bit complicated. I knew that Kruger could never be trusted at Goldfarb. A person with a divided loyalty is like a wave of the sea… unsettled… tossed by the wind. I called my lawyer, Ben. He said that if I fired him, it would appear to be a vendetta because of his testimony at my grand jury investigation when Wicked disappeared. Ben then advised me to facilitate an advance in his career… out of Memphis. Remembering Kruger's earlier comments that Memphis was just a stepping stone, I made a couple of calls to some of my Chicago friends and got him a job as a floor trader at the CBOT. He took the position and moved. Unfortunately, after he had been there for less than two weeks, he was murdered outside his condominium. Two drug dealers were recorded on a security camera as they slashed his throat. They are now serving life sentences. Kruger's family still suspects that I arranged the murder."

"Feter Sol, I am so sorry for you. I never knew any of this."

"Well, there is one more event that I might as well tell you about. Bad things often occur in threes and I had a trilogy of accusations. Wicked had a son named Shimei. Everyone called him Sammy. Well, Sammy took over the family enterprise after Wicked disappeared. He was worse than his father in so many ways. Worse alcohol abuse. Probably illegal drugs also. He also continued to try to make my life miserable. As his company faltered, he even filed a civil suit against me. The suit went nowhere but Goldfarb Fabric filed for bankruptcy and was sold off to a competitor. Having lost his family business, he sat around every day dreaming up ways to make my life miserable. He's the one most responsible for trying to link me to Kruger's murder. I talked with my friend Ben who advised me to take no actions as there was nothing to defend. Then… Sammy died unexpectedly."

"What happened to him, Feter Sol?"

"Sammy was duck hunting down in Red Panther Reserve in Issatoba County with his old gambling buddies. He went to his duck stand just before sunrise but didn't return to the lodge after the hunt. Late in the day, his hunting buddies found his body. Floating face down. He drowned in only three feet of water."

"Three feet! Was he drunk?"

"Well, he *was* at duck camp… Plime', you won't be surprised, but his mother thinks I was responsible for his death also."

Uncle Solomon glanced at me wistfully and then returned his gaze to the drops of water meandering down the glass of iced tea.

"You now understand." He took a puff from his pipe as I listened, knowing there was more. "I am just exhausted from all of the conflict. I don't want to be emotionally frisked in another ten years when the next drifter's body shows up in Nevada…. It will be better for me to get out of the public eye. Life will be simpler. I can continue to trade cotton and gold in my own account. I obviously will have more time to devote to the Asia trade. For now, I will trade here at Havilah. If things don't settle, I may move to Paris."

He turned and gazed at the lavender flowers of the wisteria. He took a sip of his iced tea.

"So much of my life has been in vain. Vanity of vanities... I spent too much time seeking an edge as a glorified peddler… chasing the wind. Money doesn't mean so much anymore… although I would hate to be without it. Titles and positions are no longer important. More than ever, I cherish personal relationships, but close relationships are a rarity for me now. I never appreciated the importance of family bonds. Now, I've been abandoned by my family, largely of my own making. Your family in Tippah County despises me. I dread going to my own office. My closest remaining ties are to you, Fritz, Ben, and Coco… I proclaimed the priorities so often for you. *God, Family, Business, and then games...* Like many experts, I am qualified to profess expertise because I have suffered from my own mistakes, created by own selfish desire."

His eyes glistened for the first time that I could recall since he played "Amazing Grace" in Tippah County.

"Feter Sol, I don't know what to say…"

"Sure you do, Plime'…. *Wisdom is more precious than rubies* and *the beginning of wisdom is the fear of the Lord.* Yes, my priorities were not right. I chose a path blinded by pride, but found humility the hard way. Looking back, there were plenty of warnings and guard rails. I can see them clearly now… but I ignored them."

***

I sat there silently as he took a sip of tea. Then with a refreshing tone, he asked, "Have I shown you the Darwinian lessons of wisteria?"

"Feter Sol, I know nothing about wisteria. What are you talking about?" I asked.

"Let's go for a short walk."

The central feature of Uncle Solomon's backyard was a pair of parallel trellises covered with wisteria. Both were in full bloom. Between the two wisteria was a white wrought-iron bench. We sat on the bench which seems to have been purposely placed for contemplation.

"Tell me what you see."

"Feter Sol, both flowering vines are beautiful. One flower is slightly darker in color than the other; both are shades of lavender. Both have been expertly trimmed. There is a gardener who is playing a very important role in keeping your backyard up so nicely. You must be paying him well. I'm sure there's something that I don't see. Why don't you just tell me?"

"These two wisteria vines either hide or display the mystery of the universe, depending on your perspective. Do you see the difference? Look closely at the vine to your right. Notice how the vine wraps around the wooden supports. In which direction does the vine twine? Clockwise or counterclockwise when viewed from below?" he asked.

I went over to the vine and inspected it more closely, now more attentive to specific detail. Yes, every vine rotated in the same direction. "I am amazed but every vine rotates clockwise. Isn't that bizarre!" I said.

"No Plime', it is not bizarre. It happens for a reason. What do you think the reason would be?"

"I know little about biology, but the pattern is so clear that it must be related to a function of environment. Perhaps the twist is related to an effort to reach sunlight. Yes, that would seem to make sense," I said.

"I like your logic. The concept of a plant turning to face the sun is called heliotropism. Now look at the plant to our left. The two wisteria vines are very similar and share the same sunlight, but they are very different. Again, I ask which way does the left vine twine?"

I carefully inspected the vine on the left and noted that it twisted in the opposite direction. "It is just the opposite. It rotates counterclockwise."

"What does that do to your sunlight theory?" Solomon asked.

"There are obviously some factors that I don't understand. Can you help me make sense of this?" I asked.

"Okay, the plant on the right, wisteria sinensis, originally came from China. The one on the left, wisteria floribunda, came from Japan. Their vines grow in opposite directions for a very good reason: they are programmed that way. It is in their DNA. How the different DNA got there is a point of conjecture, depending on your views of evolution*. But, one vine of two similar plants clearly grows clockwise and its close relative grows counterclockwise. Here in my garden, the difference has to be explained by ingrained nature and not nurture... at least not nurture in the lifetime of these plants as their environment is the same."

He lit his pipe and took a puff. His left eyebrow raised. "Wouldn't it be nice if human beings were programmed to always grow the right way? But no..." another puff... "we have choice which often sends us in the wrong direction."

I saw the vines from a different perspective. A bumblebee buzzed over the flowering vines. Two doves suddenly lit on the trellis and contributed their peaceful "coo." I imagined a distant crunch of gravel. I heard no belligerent crows.

"That's enough about polar bears and wisteria for today. Let's not even discuss gold or Southeast Asia. Go home to your family. Hug your wife and kids. I will drop you a note later about managing the Asia trade," said Uncle Solomon.

I went home and spent the afternoon with the wife and my boys. Uncle Solomon joined us in Jackson for our Protestant church service. Interestingly, the sermon was about priorities of life... with no mention of polar bears or wisteria.

One other thing: the dental records were compared. The skeletal remains were not Wicked's.

GOD, Family, business... and then games.

*[One theory is that the DNA of Japanese wisteria was "laid down" before the tectonic plate shift that "pushed" Japan from the southern to the northern hemisphere. If so, the *south-of-the-equator* counter-clockwise DNA pre-existed the tectonic shift and appears to have been made "permanent..." although time is relative regarding tectonic shifts.]

C. RANDLE VOYLES MD

9 A PEDDLER'S INSIGHT

June, 1988.
The follow-up letter from Uncle Sol planning the Asia trade.

Dear Plimenick,

I am an old cotton trader. I have earned several other not-so-glorious titles, including an accused murderer. More recently, you have teased me with the title of General Systems Theorist. Accepting that the latter title may have some applicability, let's peer into the future and design an optimal trading system for the Asian trade. Our goals are longevity and consistent profits over time.

We must *protect* the mutual funds. They are to us what a brush is to a painter. They must be profitable; otherwise, they will no longer exist. Like any other business, their profits are based on revenue minus expenses. Gross revenue is primarily a function of total size of the fund: bigger is better, as the fund takes a percentage of total assets on an annual basis.

The fund generates expenses at many levels. They obviously have to advertise to sell their funds; brokers and marketing cost them money. In an effort to garner more deposits, they may offer "teaser" benefits such as no front-end load fees, "low-loads" and no restrictions on frequency of trades. Some funds are experimenting with a shared platform for various families of funds; the daughter companies will share their fees with the mothership, seeking a smaller piece of a larger pie.

The fund portfolio must maintain a level of liquidity which will provide cash for new investments as well as redemptions. If they keep their cash too high, they have less money working in the market. If they keep the cash too low, redemptions will mandate selling stocks at a disadvantageous time. We must design our strategy in light of their constraints.

Our critics may label us as market timers, but we will strive to be gentle market timers. Here are some suggested parameters:

1) Limit trade size to a small percentage (<0.25%) of each fund's total assets.
2) When strong signals occur, spread out trades over multiple funds. Obviously, we will have to define what a strong signal is. I suggest that we delve into Kruger's technical factors with trendlines, etc.
3) Limit frequency of purchases; avoid "noisy" buy signals. We should set a goal to purchase any one fund no more often than every 4 weeks.
4) Prolong holding period (remember buying is 50%; selling is 80%).
5) Buy with enough size to mitigate nominal exchange fees if they are present. Simple arithmetic will suffice here. Fortunately, the fund managers keep these fees low to entice new buyers.
6) Study each fund to identify less actively traded funds (higher loads are generally associated with less turnover). These "sleepy funds" may be more tolerant of trading frequency if you maintain a healthy balance in the family's money market.
7) Plan for trading inefficiencies to be eliminated.
8) Entertain margin for less speculative trades.

Remember: Wisdom is more precious than rubies. Monitor your own white box and never lose your priorities: GOD, Family, business, and then games.

Sincerely,

Feter Solomon

Without revealing further proprietary information, Uncle Solomon's view of the future was insightful. He implemented our trading system while I continued our studies of the "white box" of the world. We observed that many Southeast Asian funds correlated more closely with moves in the NASDAQ than the S&P 500. At the same time, the Hang Seng index of Hong Kong reflected a significant percentage of property stocks and the funds were quite interest rate sensitive. The Lunar New Year of Asia also provided significant opportunities as individual markets were closed for varying lengths. (The holidays were celebrated over 3 to 8 days, varying by country. Meanwhile daily asset prices were assigned according to the most recent working day, occasionally 3-4 days stale). While rising tides raise all boats, Asian trading tides "catch up" with the rest of the financial world upon re-opening after the Lunar New Year festivities.

Kuala Lumpur was a success by any measure and never experienced a loss in a single quarter. While the system worked for more than a decade, it came to an abrupt end in a devastating night with Big Sue.

10 A NIGHT WITH BIG SUE

A decade later…
50 years old
March, 2001
Chicago

Big Sue is her nickname. She is the world's largest and most complete Tyrannosaurus rex ever found. Forty feet long, she is a permanent feature at the Field Museum of Natural History in Chicago. Sue is an example that the world does evolve. She and her closest relatives are now extinct. Ironically, it was Uncle Solomon's trading system named Kuala Lumpur that was about to become extinct… in the shadow of Big Sue. The year was 2001; it marked the peak of the "irrationally exuberant" bubble in technology.

MasterFund Company offered an invitation-only seminar in Chicago for their high-volume investors and traders. Saturday evening's event was at the Field Museum. We had cocktails on the street side of Sue followed by dinner on the lakeside. At the dinner, my assigned seat backed up next to the huge skeletal display of the large dinosaur. To my right was seated my Uncle Solomon. To my left was John Towery, the chief operations officer of MasterFund Company. I had planned a specific line of inquiry for the evening and was quick to initiate conversation with upper management.

"What a delightful evening and wonderful setting. The American College of Surgeons meets in Chicago every three or four years. I've presented at the McCormick Center on several occasions," I said with a casual stroke of my ego. "However, this is my first time to visit the museum. My uncle and I are appreciative of you and your company. You seem to be always on the cutting edge of industry."

"Doctor, we at MasterFund are honored to have you and your uncle. We have both benefited from your trading strategies," said Towery. "The world continues to change, and we at the company have to adapt. It is apropos that we are sitting next to the great dinosaur who has been named Sue."

"You may or may not know my uncle's trading system. Ironically, it is based on evolution… evolution in the mutual fund industry with sector funds," I said. *Didn't that sound pompous?* I continued. "One dinosaur fades out, and a more resilient creature blazes a new path. It seems the same with trading systems. We named our trading system Kuala Lumpur as we focused on the markets of Southeast Asia."

"Cute," said Towery.

"I have a question for you. One of my uncle's mutual fund trades was recently declined. In explanation, one of your trading associates suggested that the fund was temporarily closed in consideration of charging new fees for short-term redemptions. Is there any substance to that?"

"Doctor, as you know as well as anyone in this room, we created our MasterFund collection of international funds with the long-term investor in mind. We charged nominal transaction fees. In our competitive market, we wanted to provide the widest range of products and still be investor friendly."

"You have been innovators for the industry," I said.

"Yes, our growth has been exponential. A large number of family funds added their produce to our platform. In the process, we inadvertently created an overly convenient vehicle for hot money from market-timers and day-traders. Early on, the market-timers made little difference as buyers frequently offset sellers. However, an increasing number of large hedge funds have piled on with one-sided action in recent times. Thus, we have no choice. We are implementing new rules. We will impose fees for short-term redemptions and restrictions on the frequency of trades."

I was not surprised by the message, but I was surprised that the COO was the messenger.

"But don't despair," Towery said. "Tomorrow morning, we are introducing better vehicles for traders with short-term holding patterns. They are called exchange traded funds or ETFs. That's why you've been invited. You will need a new trading system. Kuala Lumpur will become extinct on Monday... just like Big Sue."

At that moment, a waiter in his tuxedo approached our table. He must have noted a sense of anguish in my face. "Sir, may I refresh your ice tea?"

"No sir. Could I please have a Balvenie? Make that a double..."

***

Later in the evening. Elbows resting on the balcony railing just outside the museum. Uncle Solomon and I had full stomachs and dizzied heads. The breeze whipped off Lake Michigan. The mist in our faces was refreshing. A tugboat churned the water in a struggle to push a barge.

"Feter Sol, you are right again. Inefficiencies in the marketplace get worked out."

"Plimenik, as Towery said, we played the window well but that window has been shut. I suspect over-zealous traders radically disrupted the fund managers' ecosystems. The whale-hunters broke the rules that we established for Kuala Lumpur. MasterFund had no choice. That's evolution in finance! Kuala Lumpur was declared dead at the foot of Big Sue..."

Another blustery wind followed. The tugboat foghorn blared as the engine groaned. Uncle Solomon tried to light his pipe and took a signature pause. With the flash of his lighter, I could see the raised eyebrow, heralding another Solomon soliloquy.

"Did you know that the Ice Age is thought to have come on abruptly... destroyed Big Sue's ecosystem... some say a large meteorite struck earth... precipitating 'global cooling'..."

I stood there quietly enjoying his contemplative mood, anticipating more. The seemingly lack-of-connectedness always made perfect sense to me... after a lifetime of mentorship.

"Big Sue's ecosystem was radically disrupted," he said. "We scavengers of finance need not complain."

Another cool breeze whipped a refreshing spray from the surface of Lake Michigan. Yes, Feter Sol had predicted this day from early in our venture. Inefficiencies in finance, once exploited, tend to be corrected through better mousetraps or regulation.

"One dinosaur fades out," I proclaimed, "but a new creature will emerge. There will be a new dragon to slay. We'll blaze a new trail. We will succeed again!"

"Plime', take a rest." I was suddenly interrupted by Uncle Sol. "Take a break from even thinking about finance. I hate to say it, but you remind me of the youthful Kruger. Your success has rendered you vulnerable— vulnerable to quick losses. Preserving a nest egg can be more difficult than gathering it. It's time to re-assess the priorities of old. Thank God for our good run." He turned and faced me. "Enjoy your family; you have a lovely wife and two great sons. Focus on your teaching. Work on your academic projects. Put your trading game aside..."

"Your advice has always been sound, and I have tried to follow it. However, I feel like Pavlov's dog after the last decade. Surely there will be another system to become available," I said knowing that the opportunity may or may not be there.

"Wait. Be patient," he repeated. "You are vulnerable in times of change."

"Yes Sir, prudence is the word."

Per Uncle Sol's direction, I moved all positions to cash. However, I immediately began to search for other ideas. *Surely this is not the end for a trading Maestro, a mathematician extraordinaire, a brain that is hard to contain.* But on further thought, I recognized that I was just a small-town general surgeon who made a single serendipitous observation that was then harnessed by an insightful uncle – an uncle with the humility to label himself as a glorified peddler. As expected, I received a letter a few days later -- three-hole punched – yes, to be added to Uncle Sol's cherished three-ring binder. The style was exactly the same as the first letters I received at the Falkner train station thirty years previously.

Don't wear yourself out to get rich.
Be wise enough to know when to quit.
In the blink of an eye wealth disappears,
for it will sprout wings
and fly away like an eagle.

Mishlei 23: 4-5

11 PARIS THROUGH A KALEIDOSCOPE

7 years later…
My age: 58 years
October, 2008

It was not for lack of trying, but I never discovered another "poor man's arbitrage." My wheels never again achieved any real traction: spin, spun, spent. I was frustrated… but not as much as the invested public during the financial crisis of 2007-2008. Uncle Solomon invited me to Paris suggesting I would benefit from personal reflection in the City of Light. I accepted his invitation. Typical for Feter Sol, he had planned the itinerary.

"Plimenik, Paris offers many lessons. We shall learn from others. We will look through a historical lens. Bring your walking shoes."

On the first morning after a fitful jet-lagged sleep, Uncle Solomon met me in the lobby of the Ritz at Place Vendome. "Shall we have coffee here? This is such a grand hotel," I asked.

"Heaven forbid! Every moment is precious, and I have an even more special breakfast planned."

We negotiated the tourist-clogged path from the Ritz to the renowned coffee shop named Angelina on rue de Rivoli. Uncle Solomon ordered the specialty drink (thick hot chocolate called "The African"). As if on cue, he launched into his Socratic soliloquy.

"This was the stomping ground for the late Coco Chanel as she changed fashion for the world. At the height of her career, she lived at the hotel where you stayed last night. Every morning, she took our walk to this reserved table where she had this very same hot chocolate known as 'The African.' She lived a life of supposed grandeur, elegance, and glamor… but her ego led to your first Parisian case study."

He took a sip of his chocolate.

"Coco took on a business partner to help finance a new perfume product which ultimately became known as Chanel #5. Needless to say, the venture was enormously successful, but Coco became distraught when she saw how much profit went to her business partner. She felt that she had been cheated. She sued her partner and lost. Fast forward a half century. Coco is dead, and the entire Chanel Enterprise is owned by the offspring of Coco's business partner. By the way, their name is Wertheimer… I think they are my cousins."

"Cousins?" I asked.

"Perhaps, at least distantly. Don't you think Coco reinforces some old lessons?"

"Feter Sol, for sure. As a prime case study, one must conclude that the borrower is slave to the lender. Coco should have appreciated that wisdom is more precious than rubies."

"Plime', your memory serves you well. There is nothing new under the sun," he responded. "Paris offers many examples from lessons of the past. Man's nature has not changed in thousands of years. We will learn from others, especially when we look through a historical lens…"

Our next stop was Notre Dame.

Uncle Solomon gave a remarkably detailed tour of the Gothic structure completed in the 1300s. I was surprised that he knew so much about the architecture and construction of the cathedral, but I found his historic perspective even more fascinating. Several other tourists eavesdropped as he pontificated like a tour guide.

"The Church was central to life in the Paris of the Middle Ages. However, man's errant ways crept into Church practices. The all-powerful priests began accepting generous payments in exchange for granting indulgences that supposedly would save the sinner's soul. The greedy priests apparently did not heed the old Hebrew proverb that riches will not help on the day of judgment. Thus, we have another case study of the frailty of man as there is nothing new under the sun."

The nearby tourists leaned in.

"The decay of the Church hierarchy only worsened and precipitated the Protestant Reformation. Martin Luther has been given credit for much of the change with his mantra of 'sola scriptura,' which means the Church should rely on 'Scripture alone'. Of course, the

Gutenberg printing press was a technologic disruptor when it made copies of the Holy Bible available to the masses."

His pensive gaze was then directed to the top of the old historic structure. I noted the raised eyebrow.

"'Sola scriptura.' There are two modern-day groups of discerning Jews who also rely on the original scripture as supreme authority. Much like the German protestors who questioned the church practices, these Jews refuse to accept the rabbi's directives and extrapolations found in the Talmud and Midrash. This first group call themselves Karaite Jews. Karaite actually means 'readers' in Hebrew and, as readers, they promote a near-literal translation in their self-determined study of the original Scripture. At a certain level, I like their perspective. The second group of 'readers' is even more interesting. They are the Messianic Jews. They also promote a literal interpretation of the Jewish Scripture, but as prophecy of the Christian New Testament. Thus, the Messianic Jews might rightly be called Karaites of sorts. You know that Judaism provided the cocoon from which Christianity erupted. In my view, the most clear prophecy in the Jewish Scripture is contained in the 53rd chapter by the prophet Isaiah."[6]

He gazed at the intricate statues of Christ and his disciples. I had an immediate flashback to my youth: that hot Tippah County day; red oak tree; Uncle Solomon's instruction to *never forget our shared Hebrew heritage*. Now, in Paris… the same message.

"But I digress…" He turned toward his newly-acquired audience of wandering tourists. "Paris offers many lessons. Take mental notes of everything you see. Look through a historical lens, maybe a prism. You will see what others don't."

---

[6] Isaiah 53: 5-9 (NLT): *But He was pierced for our rebellion, crushed for our sins. He was beaten so we could be whole. He was whipped so we could be healed. All of us, like sheep, have strayed away. We have left God's paths to follow our own. Yet the LORD laid on Him the sins of us all. He was oppressed and treated harshly, yet he never said a word. He was led like a lamb to the slaughter. And as a sheep is silent before the shearers, He did not open his mouth. Unjustly condemned, he was led away].... He had done no wrong and had never deceived anyone. But He was buried like a criminal; He was put in a rich man's grave.*

On the next day, Uncle Solomon directed us to the Eiffel tower.

"Seven million tourists visit the tower every year. Spare me the crowd. I trust you have done your research. I will want a report this evening. Look through your historical lens."

My wife and I spent most of the day around the tower. Guided tour. Unbelievable crowd, all toting cameras. I will not offer descriptive details as such is the product of guidebooks, but no one can make a first visit to the tower without being impressed. Constructed for the 1889 World's Fair, Eiffel's project was the tallest man-made structure in the world until 1930 when the Chrysler Building in New York City was completed. I took mental notes per Uncle Sol's direction. That evening, I gave what I thought was an insightful overview of Eiffel's feat of engineering. Uncle Sol listened attentively.

"Is that all you have to report?" he asked. "The Eiffel Tower represents another fabulous case study. I would have assumed that you would have looked through your financial prism. How was the tower financed?"

"My assumption is that the World's Fair paid for the tower. Am I wrong?"

"Plime', you are partly wrong and partly right. The French authorities put up less than 20% of the estimated cost. Gustave Eiffel created his own company to fund the rest. In the agreement, he received all income generated by the tower for the next 20 years." He paused and grinned. "He recovered his costs in the first year." Then he raised his left eyebrow. "Brings to mind two old Hebrew admonitions: 'wealth is the crown of the wise' and 'good people leave an inheritance to their children's children.' But Plime', the most valuable inheritance cannot be measured with numbers. For the inheritance that really counts, there are no numbers. However, an Eiffel family company managed the tower until 1980."

He took a sip of his Balvenie.

"If Gustave were here tonight, we would have to declare him an honorary member of our Scavengers of Commerce Club. True talent extends beyond borders and time! Here's to our friend Gustave and the Club!"

He clinked his glass to mine causing an errant splash. Reflexively, he wiped up the splatter with his finger and licked it dry. "Ahh, a quote

from Faulkner comes to mind. 'Pouring out liquor is like burning books.'"
Of course, he followed with a self-congratulatory chuckle.

"Plime', Eiffel is a great case study, and you are a great student.
Always have been. I remember how attentive you were back in Tippah
County. Those were such hot days."

"And I remember to this day one of your statements. 'Good
business is based on math and science and then psychology. Numbers
count, but your life is more than a balance sheet.'"

"Plime', you do remember well, but there is much more to learn
from this trip to Paris. To truly learn, you must look through a historical
lens, maybe a prism… better yet, even a kaleidoscope."

In the ensuing days, I visited the traditional tourist attractions:
Versailles, the Louvre, Museum D'Orsay, Les Invalides, and the Arc de
Triomphe. On the last afternoon, I followed the crowds up to Montmartre,
the highest hill which overlooks Paris. I then ascended to a higher point,
up the stairs of the domed Basilica of the Sacre Coeur. *The most magnificent
view of Paris!* Exhausted from the adventure, I made my way to Uncle
Solomon's flat where he met me at the door.

"I know you have walked all day, but let's take a short stroll to my
favorite bench at Parc Monceau." It was late in the afternoon, and I was as
"wore out" as any Tippah County dirt farmer. However, I relished the
thought of a one-on-one review with my dear uncle. We strolled through
the ornate gate of the nearby park. The Arc de Triomphe stood majestically
in the distance. Making our way between the joggers and the nannies with
their strollers, we took a rest on an enamel-green bench next to a reflection
pond shouldered by Grecian columns from another era. Another case
study in the making… Feter Sol began his overview.

"Can you imagine the grandeur that Napoleon must've sensed as
he redesigned the entire city? This very park at one time was set aside only
for the French Royals. Napoleon opened it as a public park. Parc
Monceau… Do you see that there is nothing new under the sun?"

"Feter Sol, this park is filled with symbols of the past. We walked
over the arched bridge that looks like the Rialto in Venice. Some creative
artisan added a small Egyptian pyramid. A Roman dome marks the major
entrance. Even Napoleon's Arc de Triomphe, just outside the gates, is a
design embellished from the Roman past."

"Parc Monceau offers a wide variety of case studies, but let's start with Napoleon and the Arc de Triomphe," he said. "He designed it as the most grandiose structure to commemorate his military success. He commissioned the building of it, but he never saw the completed Arc, except from his position in a coffin. He died a lonely death in exile on a distant island in the southern Atlantic Ocean. He dreamed big and was very effective for a long period. Paradoxically, Hitler had a more glorious but short-lived victory parade through the Arc during World War II. But that is remote history." He lit his pipe. I enjoyed the smell of cherry tobacco. "Paris and Parc Monceau provide a potpourri of case studies. Plime', these artifacts are cultural tombstones marking man's greed and fleeting display of earthly power. These embellished façades, forever stained by the soup of hubris, reflect the imperfections of man. Vanity. Vanity of vanities. There is nothing new under the sun."

"But Feter Sol, can we not lighten up a bit! Let's enjoy the grandeur of the moment as little Napoleons. This is my last night in Paris, and we have much to celebrate. After all, didn't we beat the market?"

"Plime', no! We did *not* beat the market. We just exploited a temporary logistical segment in the ups and downs of daily trading. Your astute observation identified the path to our Serendipity, and the markets pushed a few shekels our way. But Plime', remember, the original Serendipity was just an imaginary place in a Persian-Ceylonese fairy tale. In real life, it is a rare destination – a destination generally associated with chance. In your case, another technologic disruptor played a role. Had it not been for the advent of CNN providing your initial clue to the misprice of gold, we likely would not be here now. That reminds me of an old Hebrew proverb that we may throw the dice, but the Lord determines how they fall."

"Our returns were so good that some might claim that we played with loaded dice," I said.

"And Plime', I can imagine what your Uncle Wilbur would say. *Those gol-durned greedy speculators trading hot money like river boat gamblers… in a den of thieves.*"

"Feter Sol, rest assured, all of my kinfolk would appreciate how you used the market to teach Godly principles: 'Wisdom is more precious than rubies. Wisdom is more precious than silver and gold. The beginning of wisdom is the fear of the Lord.' You have taught me priorities: God, family, business, and then games. But still, I must confess. My upbringing in Tippah has me deeply indoctrinated in the 'sweat of the brow' mentality. Plant the crops in the spring. Provide for them as they grow. Gather the harvest in the fall and prepare for winter. Feter Sol, even in my second decade of trading international markets, I still seem more comfortable in dirty work boots... dirty work boots on my feet and a hoe in my hands working in knee-high corn. But... you were my mentor who redirected my gaze..."

"You may seem more comfortable in a corn patch, but trading markets came quite natural for you," said Uncle Solomon, "and you spotted the initial inefficiency."

A fresh breeze caused a ripple on the reflection pond. The afternoon sun bounced off the falling leaves. I felt a gratifying peace.

"Feter Sol, do you think the inefficiency was a gift from God?"

"Plime', I admire the humility of discerning introspection. As to whether the inefficiency was truly a gift of Providence, I don't have an answer. The real gift was your gift of focus. However, some might claim that your focus and dogged persistence in the hunt is more worldly than godly. But, think with me. The means and the ends are both important. After a bountiful harvest, you must not change your life's priorities. God first, then family. As we age, business and games become less important. Every new phase of life presents a new set of challenges and conflict. Conflict respects no age."

Two joggers ran by. A young mother pushed her baby stroller. A pigeon landed near my feet and cocked his head as if he recognized the wisdom of my Feter Sol.

"Plimenik, never forget the instructions from that three-ringed binder. By now, you must recognize that the instructions are not unique... not from me. They are from an early uncle of mine. His name was also Solomon. At best, I am my uncle's parrot; at worst, his plagiarist. My Uncle Solomon prepared a prolific record of guiding principles for healthy living. However, at the end of his life, he knew he had failed his God and his people. He wrote a historic memoir, a record of his early successes and ultimate shortcomings. His memoir is titled Kohelet. I have a copy for you." He retrieved the small book from his coat pocket.

"Thank you, Feter Sol. What would your Uncle Solomon advise me now?"

"In his advice, my insightful uncle would likely borrow your agricultural metaphor. You have enough grain in your crib to make the winter. Recognize the blessing. Be humble. The spring will bring time for new planting. Wait patiently for the rains. You will be sewing a different seed with a longer growth cycle. Be diligent for your DNA can entrap you like Chinese wisteria. Read my uncle's memoir; he offers ancient guidelines for today's so-called value investing, as if value can be enumerated. You will recognize that Buffet and Bogle offer mere permutations of my uncle's earlier directives. Be your own Karaite and don't lose focus. Maintain your priorities. They should never change. You are more than a glorified peddler."

[The specific guidelines with Feter Sol's translations are recorded in the references of this book.]

He retrieved a paper bag from his pocket and tossed sunflower seeds to the pigeon. "Plime', have you ever seen a full field of sunflowers? They all turn in unison throughout the day as their glorious yellow heads follow the path of the sun."

"I know, Feter Sol. It is more of heliotropism. Sunflowers are programed to do that. It's in their DNA." I gazed beyond the reflection pool. Looking through a complex lens, I saw the past through the present, or was it the present through the past? The artifacts of Parc Monceau were just feeble efforts of man's attempt to embellish points of vanishing grandeur. There are important lessons from Parc Monceau, perhaps most clearly observed through the kaleidoscope of my Uncle Solomon(s)...

***

On the flight home, I read the memoir named Kohelet. My uncle's uncle knew wisdom, wealth, and power... but in the end, he self-destructed. His DNA provided the opportunity for errant choice and he lost focus of the Sun.

***

Here is a cogent review of Kohelet by Thomas Wolfe (1900-1938).

"For of all I have ever seen or learned, this book seems to me the noblest, the wisest, and the most powerful expression of man's life upon this earth – and also the highest flower of poetry, eloquence, and truth. I am not given to dogmatic judgments in the matter of literary creation, but if I had to make one I could say that this book is the greatest single piece of writing I have ever known, and the wisdom expressed in it the most lasting and profound."

12 BACK TO TIPPAH

Goldfarb Cotton, the one-time stalwart of the Memphis cotton trade, dissolved with Uncle Solomon's departure. At first, he retreated to his home in east Memphis where he traded cotton and gold in his personal account and managed our fund called Kuala Lumpur until it ended. It is sad to me how my once out-going socialite mentor had become a recluse. His perception was that his respect in the Memphis community had been destroyed. Even his mannerisms -- his professorial posturing, the raised eyebrow -- became a thing of the past. In its place was a bland and blank facial masking. "Both Christian and Jewish friends treated me, once again, as a leper. I felt like General Ulysses Grant had nailed personal Edict 11 to my front door." (Original reference to Grant in Chapter 7).

Uncle Solomon spent progressively more time in Paris. Finally, he sold Havilah and moved to a Haussmann flat in the 8th arrondissement, rue de Monceau. He and Coco enjoyed travel, taking several trans-Atlantic cruises to Canada, never setting foot again in the US. They took most of the river cruises in Europe, the last one being from Bucharest to Budapest. They also took the Mekong River cruise to Cambodia as well as the Yangtze River cruise in China. In spite of their differences in age, Coco remained the faithful compatriot of Uncle Solomon. You must understand that the lifespan of a Parisian modelling career is short even though she still turns heads as she walks her one-eyed dog in Parc Monceau. Of course, that brutish canine is named Uncle Wilbur.

In November, 2009, I received the dreaded phone call. A call from Paris. Coco. News of the fate of all mortals. She and Uncle Solomon had just returned to Paris from a trans-Atlantic cruise. One of the stops on their itinerary was Iceland; Uncle Sol was determined to visit the famous Blue Lagoon, a geological wonder where tourists dip in the silica-rich, naturally-warmed waters. Uncle Solomon suffered a syncopal episode as he exited the waters, but he immediately improved and refused medical evaluation. He also experienced "indigestion" while completing the strenuous walk to the Plains of Abraham in Quebec City. He had no further difficulties until he arrived at his flat in Paris where he sustained another syncopal episode and cardiac arrest. Efforts at resuscitation were not successful.

As no surprise to me, Uncle Solomon had made explicit plans for his funerary particulars. Small memorial service. Jewish synagogue in Marais (eastern Paris). His body was to be cremated. As a specific directive, I was to take his ashes and spread them over Aunt Grace's grave at Pine Hill. In explanation, he wanted to spare me the potential anguish of negotiating with the Primitive Baptists about the formal burial of a Jew in a Christian cemetery. He then challenged me - in typical fashion for my Feter Sol, even posthumously - to study the disappointment of Niccolo Matas in Florence, Italy. *Niccolo Matas?* Who might that be? Here is what I found. According to Wikipedia, Matas was a Jewish architect who designed the magnificent marble façade of the famous cathedral known as Basilica de Santa Croce (contains the funerary monuments of Michelangelo, Galileo, others). Matas requested to be buried inside the Basilica with the Italian heroes as a tribute to his architectural expertise, but because he was a Jew, his request was denied. He was buried under an outside step.

Also, typical for Uncle Solomon, he sent his ashes in an urn graced with the Star of David on one side and a Christian Cross on the other. Written on an attached envelope were his instructions to read the enclosed letter at Pine Hill only after his ashes had been spread over Aunt Grace's grave. Here's the letter:

Dear Plimenik,

Paris may be the City of Light, but for me mornings are most celebrated. My favorite place to behold the break of a new day is from the highest Parisian hill which we know as Montmartre, the site of the Basilica de Sacre Couer. Can you see it through my eyes? The sun peeks over the horizon and lifts the morning mist, thus exposing the artifacts of man's achievement: Notre Dame reflects the glory of the Medieval church; the Louvre reflects the glory of French Royals; the Arc de Triomphe, the glory of the Napoleonic emperor; the tower of Eiffel, the glory of capitalism.

On any given day, I am choked by a mass of humanity struggling under the sun... a mass in a hurry... a mass seeking its own achievement...

seeking ephemeral monetary return… seeking pleasure. In the masses, I see myself. I have chased the wind. For what? Vanity. Vanity of vanities. I see the sun rise in the east and settle in the west, only to repeat the next morning. The Seine flows from left to right and finally out to sea, but the sea is never full. I reflect on my life. The successes. The failures. In the end, both reflect a chasing of the wind. Vanity of vanities.

Now with my ashes spread on the sacred soil of Tippah County, allow me to continue my final introspection. I truly enjoyed the labor of conquest in the marketplace as well as the fruits of my labor. I rewarded myself with good food, great wines, and hearty laughter in the company of bought friends at my multi-columned mansion. I knew carnal pleasure. I denied myself nothing. Yes, these were the rewards of my financial prowess. Now I sit here as a lonely man overlooking artifacts of previous French wealth. Like the Royals, I never appreciated what was enough. Even in modern times, those who love money never have enough. Don't the wise, the wealthy, and the day laborer all face the same fate? Are they not all chasing the wind? I have concluded that it is better to be content in your work as you face your day-to-day challenges but take time to enjoy your food and drink; these are gifts from the hand of God. Just as there is a time for every season, there is a time to work but there also is a time to rest.

Plime', life is not fair. There is a randomness to success as the path to any Serendipity is poorly marked, if at all. We both struggled to elucidate the white boxes of life, but no one knows the future. The wise do not necessarily prosper just as the strong don't necessarily win the battle. Chance happens to all of them… and to all of us. In spite of the greatest effort of man, no one can contain the wind. Again, enjoy the fruits of your labor but remember that God will hold you accountable for everything you do.

> With my undying love,
> Feter Sol
> PS: I told you I would die before I returned to Tippah County!

What a splendid afternoon it was. Flickering shadows from the late-afternoon sunlight rippled across the lichen-speckled tombstones. I reread my Feter Sol's eulogy. I imagined the aroma of his cherry tobacco. I could see his professorial posturing in typical soliloquy. His linen jacket.

European flare. The raised eye brow. In the rustling of leaves, I heard Feter Sol's soft whisper from decades ago:

Never forget our shared Hebrew heritage.

13 SECRETS HIDDEN IN FULL VIEW

What have you just read? How much is fiction? How much is real? Was it just a fact-filled novella? I confess; I was influenced by my neighborhood author. He suggested that "a writer needs three things: *experience, observation,* and *imagination*, any two of which, at times any one of which, can supply the lack of the others."

As to *experience*, the outlined market inefficiency was real; the dates and manner of discovery were real; the detail of implementation was described with intended clarity. Kuala Lumpur was a rewarding endeavor. Finally, the demise of Kuala Lumpur at the foot of Big Sue was only minimally embellished. Market timing of mutual funds is still possible but not likely to be profitable in view of punitive fees for early redemptions.

As to *observation*, yes, I had the rich uncle. The photograph on the dedication page is real and authentic. Can you see the upturned eyebrow? As had previously been suggested by Faulkner, every time I lifted his eyebrow, my Feter Sol did all the talking. I did my best to record his instruction precisely, but on occasion my memory was aided by the mythopoeic prism of a Parisian kaleidoscope. And you are right, Feter Sol's name was altered as a matter of editorial privilege.

As to *imagination*… I found it a useful tool, especially when sprinkled with plagiarism. I sense no literary guilt of copycat, for what modern day writing is truly original? Didn't my early Uncle Solomon(s) say *there is nothing new under the sun?* Furthermore, Faulkner said that a writer, if he is a good one, will not hesitate to rob from his mother. If one decides to plagiarize, selecting a good story, perhaps one that has persisted for 3000 years, would have merit. Didn't our Nobel Prize laureate write a novel named *Absalom, Absalom?* Didn't he say the only thing worth writing about is conflict in the human soul? Lift another veil! Encounter the verities of life.

A brief historical account of the original Uncle Solomon

Long ago in the land between the Euphrates River and the Red Sea, a shepherd boy named David killed a Philistine giant named Goliath... with just a stone and a sling. He subsequently won many battles and became king of a nation for the Twelve Tribes of Israel. Although referred to as the man after God's own heart, he had many faults. He took wives out of political convenience and saw marriage as conquest. Never content, he had an adulterous relationship with the wife of one of his own generals. The wife's name was Bathsheba, and their subsequent offspring was named **Solomon** (my Feter Sol's namesake).

Being a king of great pride and ambition, the aging David continued to lead his men to battle in spite of his passing years. In his last skirmish with the Philistines, he became so "weak and exhausted" that he was almost killed by a young giant named Ishbi-Benob (2 Samuel 21: 15-17). His men must have recognized the physical limitations of the aging warrior-king for they rescued him at the last moment and then banned him from the battle field, thus recording what was perhaps the first forced retirement in history. David's subsequent writings exude motor disorder, leading some to suggest that he had a progressive neurodegenerative process much like Parkinson's disease.[7] (By coincidence, Feter Sol's father, also named David, died with Parkinson's disease.)

Three thousand years ago, King David recorded the document that we know as the book called Psalms. He most likely encouraged son Solomon to compile a series of life instructions called Michlei (Proverbs in English). Solomon became a prolific writer-poet and compiled 1005 songs. His currently recognized works in addition to Proverbs include his memoire called Ecclesiastes and the poetry of Song of Solomon (SOS).

[7] King David, Son of Jesse: World's first patient with Parkinson's Disease. Journal of the Mississippi State Medical 55: 14-18. 2014.

Prince Solomon's older half-brothers anticipated becoming the next king after David. However, because of the overbearing influence of Bathsheba, the crown was promised to Solomon. Apparently recognizing that they were to be passed over, the older brothers rebelled and attempted insurrection. Absalom, the oldest son at the time, temporarily took over Jerusalem, but he was ultimately killed – against David's specific instructions – by a general named **Joab**. The next son **Adonijah** also attempted to take the throne by deception, but his effort was recognized and thwarted by Bathsheba.

If one takes the biblical account as chronologically accurate, Solomon's first regal orders led to the execution of three adversaries (1 Kings 2:1-46). These names should be familiar: **Adonijah, Joab,** and **Shimei.** *(Isn't that bizarre! The trio had the same proper names as Wicked, Kruger, and Sammy.)* King Solomon did not personally execute them. The executions were carried out by his trusted confidant named **Benaiah.** *(Now, even more bizarre! King Solomon probably knew him as Ben.)*

Thus with just a bit of imaginative transfer, the parallel protagonist to my Feter Sol could have been King Solomon from 3000 years ago. *(Did my Feter Sol just borrow the names… or more than that… borrow the plot? Was he just a copycat? How many times did he relate that there is nothing new under the sun? Does his story carry a more vicious twist than wisteria?)* Late in his life, King Solomon failed the instruction of God and ignored his own instructions from his Proverbs *(much like my Feter Sol)*. King Solomon lived his remaining life in despair, knowing that his personal failure would lead to the division of the nation of Israel. Hopefully, the *proverbial* reflections from Uncle Solomon(s) will be more useful to you.

How does Feter Sol's Coco fit in the story? **Abishag Shunami** was her original Egyptian name. In the more ancient record, there was another Abishag. Interestingly, she was from a town called Shunam. As recorded from Scripture, "King David was now old and stricken in years; and they covered him with clothes, but he gat no heat." His servants sought a young virgin… to stand before him… and to "lie in the bosom" of King David to keep him warm (1st Kings 1:1-4 KJV). The young girl's name was Abishag the Shunammite.

After David died, Solomon was crowned and Adonijah (King Solomon's older half-brother who had been passed over for the throne) asked for Abishag the Shunammite to be his wife as a compensatory prize.

King Solomon declared that such a woeful request represented an overt claim to the throne, and he had his half- brother Adonijah executed by Benaiah (1st Kings 2:23-25).

The Abishag-related Scripture perhaps does not end there. Ecclesiastes, the king's late-in-life memoir, is followed by a perplexing work of poetry called Song of Solomon. Theologians for the most part remain puzzled by its inclusion in Scripture, as the literal interpretation relates a sensuous and steamy love story seemingly devoid of religious material. Accordingly many scholars explain SOS as allegory, suggesting that SOS represents a depiction of the love of Yahweh for the nation of Israel or the love of Christ for the Church. Others explain the poetry as a beautiful depiction of a couple's love; of course, that would be a married couple. Perhaps a more literal interpretation is in order. Perhaps SOS is an extension of Solomon's memoir… an extension in a quimsical poetic format. As such SOS might describe a young Solomon's yearnings and later royal wedding to his father David's concubine named Abishag the Shunammite. A supporting clue in SOS 6:13 is reference to the bride's home in Shulam. Many scholars agree that "Shulam" (SOS 6:13) is synonymous with "Shunam" of 1 Kings. Furthermore, as would be consistent with para-Ecclesiastical theme, the marriage to Abishag in SOS represents another *vanity of vanities*. Why? Abishag would be wife number sixty-one in a line of seven hundred (1Kings 11: 1-3; SOS 6:13). Each of the explanations (allegory, analogy, or literal) is plausible at some level. Even to a dedicated Karaite, history continues to hide its secrets in full view.

Finally I re-direct your attention to Feter Sol's self-written eulogy. With a cursory study it is apparent that my Feter Sol borrowed every meaningful concept and metaphor directly from King Solomon's memoir that we know as Ecclesiastes. Both men had sampled all the worldly pleasures, and both ended their lives with disappointment. In writing his eulogy, my Feter Sol simply transposed an ancient "ecclesiastical" writing to a modern-day Parisian setting. The thematic lessons are the same. The instruction about the verities of life are timeless. They are worthy of your trust.

There is nothing new under the sun!

14 REFLECTIONS

Today…
Aged beyond 65 years…

Now that I am older, I appreciate a good afternoon nap. Sometimes as I close my eyes, I once again hear sounds from the days of my youth: that crunch of gravel on the country road; the soft moo of the Holstein cows; the cackle and caw of distant belligerent crows; the peaceful whistle of Grandpa Norton as he gathers morning eggs. A half century has changed so much. Only recently, I visited the home place, the first time in years. I was surprised to find that the old train station at Falkner is no longer; even the train rails have been removed. Old Colonel Falkner might agree with his great-grandson that the past is not yet dead, but its superficial façade, the scratched patina of humanity, has certainly changed in his namesake community.

I continued the path toward home and, I must confess, I sensed disappointment as the old gravel road had been covered with asphalt. When I rounded the curve to the home place, I was even more distressed. The giant red oak tree was gone. The new homeowner, an elderly lady still dressed in her morning seersucker robe, was hacking away at the residual vines of the wisteria around the rotting red oak stump.

"What happened to the old oak tree?" I asked.

"It died 2 years ago."

"Lightning get it?"

"Naw, it was nature but not from a storm. It was the nature of this dang wisteria. Chokin' vine put a smothering stranglehold on my tree," she said. "It didn't have a chance."

"By the way," I asked, "which way did the vine twine?"

"Oh, it rotated clockwise if you are looking from below. It's one of them Chinese wisteria. They all grow that way. You can't change 'em. They can choke the crap out of a boa constrictor. Why do you think I am out here with my hoe?"

Stock Trading Rules of Kohelet
(Ecclesiastes 11: 1-7 NLT)

11:1 Send your grain across the seas; in time, profits will flow back to you.
>*Translated: Cautiously invest long-term in overseas markets.*
>*Comparative advantage is an ancient concept.*

11:2 Divide your investments among many places, for you do not know what risk might lie ahead.
>*Translated: Diversification is obvious message.*
>*Risk tolerance decreases as a function of age.*

11:3 When clouds are heavy, the rains come down.
>*Translated: Avoid buying over-bought markets. Don't chase.*
>*Assess debt level of entity to seek "value."*
>*Remember: the borrower is slave to lender.*

11:4 Whether a tree falls north or south, it stays where it falls.
>*Translated: Once a stock falls to a critical level, it seldom recovers.*
>*Don't buy stocks that fall below $5/share.*
>*Don't catch a falling knife.*

11:5 He who keeps watching the wind will never sow;
He who keeps looking at the clouds will never reap.
>*Translated: Act on your signals; do not sit on losses.*
>*Translated #2: Discern noise from major trends: seek value.*
>*Take special care about source of your information.*

11:7 Sow your seed in the morning, at noon time, and until the evening;
You don't know which will succeed.
>*Translation is self-evident: If you choose this path, put in the necessary work.*
>*Choose fertile soil and the right seed.*
>*Provide long-term oversight and care.*

11:6 Just as you don't know the way of the wind, you don't know the work of God.
>*Translation is self-evident: You are just a glorified peddler.*
>*Maintain priorities: God, family, business, games.*

>*[#6 and #7 are intentionally out of order.]*

15 REFERENCES

Quotes from Uncle Solomon

"There is nothing new under the sun." Ecclesiastes 1:9.

"Wisdom is more precious than rubies." Proverbs 3:15.

"Wisdom is more profitable than silver, and her wages are better than gold." Proverbs 3:14.

"The beginning of wisdom is the fear of the Lord. Proverbs 1:7.

"Don't rejoice when your enemies fall; don't be happy when they stumble. For the Lord will be displeased with you." Proverbs 24: 17 – 18

"The borrower can become a slave to the lender." Proverbs 22:7.

"How much better to get wisdom than gold, to choose understanding rather than silver!" "Fire test the purity of silver and gold, but the Lord tests the heart." Proverbs 16:16; Proverbs 17:23.

"Don't wear yourself out trying to get rich. The wise enough to know when to quit. In the blink of an eye wealth disappears, for it will sprout wings and fly away like an eagle." Proverbs 23:4-5.

"Riches will not help on the day of judgment." Proverbs 11:4.

"Wealth is the crown of the wise." Proverbs 14:24.

"Good people leave an inheritance to their children's children." Prov 13:22.

"Hoarding riches harms the saver." Ecclesiastes 5:13

Quotes from Uncle James (half-brother of Jesus) addressed to the Twelve Tribes of Israel

Be sure that your faith is in God alone. Do not waiver, for a person with divided loyalty is as unsettled as a wave of the sea that is blown and tossed by the wind. James 1:6.

Temptation comes from within – from our own desires. James 1:14.

Wherever there is selfish ambition, there you will find disorder but Wisdom from above is pure... peace-loving... gentle. James 3: 16-17.

Life is like the morning fog—it's here for a little while, then gone. James 4:14.

Consider the farmers who patiently wait for the rains in the fall and in the spring. They eagerly look for the valuable harvest to ripen. You, too, must be patient. James 5:7.

Quotes from Faulkner

"You cannot swim for new horizons until you have courage to lose sight of the shore."

"Shoot high… Try to be better than yourself."

"The only thing worth writing about is the human heart in conflict with itself."

"Pouring out liquor is like burning books."

"No battle is ever won. Victory is an illusion of philosophers and fools."

"A writer needs three things: experience, observation, and imagination, any two of which, at times any one of which, will supply the lack of others."

"The past is not dead. It's not even past."

"The best fiction is better than any journalism."

"Get it down. Take chances. It may be bad, but it's the only way you can do anything good."

Other creative writing by Voyles, available from Amazon or the website: www.crvoyles.com

King David: Parkinson's First Hero. 2015

Parkinson's disease was present for ages before it was named by the Englishman. Forensic evidence is presented in this text that supports David as the first recognizable person with Parkinson's disease. Furthermore, King David proclaimed seven rules for better living with Parkinson's disease that are just as real today as they were 3000 years ago. And just perhaps... Parkinson's disease altered Western civilization.

Midnight in Florence: Splattered by Dante, Sprinkled by Faulkner. 2016.

Seeking a new direction after early retirement due to Parkinson's, the surgeon (now striving author) makes bizarre encounters in the Piazza di Santa Croce. Dante, St. Francis, Lorenzo de Medici. Was that Forrest Gump? Why does William Faulkner kept popping up? New twists are revealed on established concepts.

Adolf Hitler: Parkinson's Man of Evil, 2016.

 Adolf Hitler had Parkinson's disease and it influenced the person, if not the war. In this text, the surgeon/author "sculpted" the events of the embattled Hitler facing his demons. The presented facts are consistent with history; so is the fiction. A new insight into the mind of Hitler is offered.

Selected Technical Writing by Voyles

Electrocautery is superior to laser for laparoscopic cholecystectomy. American Journal of Surgery 160: 457, 1990.

A prospective analysis of 1518 laparoscopic cholecystectomies. The Southern Surgeons Club. New England Journal of Medicine 324: 1073-78, 1991.

Education and engineering solutions for potential problems with laparoscopic monopolar electrosurgery. American Journal of Surgery 164:57-62, 1992.

You, your patient, and the medical device industry. American Journal of Surgery 190: 178-180, 2005.

The Art and Science of Monopolar Electrosurgery. The SAGES Manual on the Fundamental Use of Surgical Energy (FUSE). 2013.

An upcoming project:

A Poor Man's Arbitrage: Goldman Sachs vs S&P 500

www.crvoyles.com

Made in the USA
Columbia, SC
02 February 2019